HURON
Grand Bend to Southampton

The schooner Sephie *beached off Kincardine's south pier, c. 1897.*

RON
Grand Bend to Southampton

SANDRA ORR

A Boston Mills Press Book

Stoddart

Canadian Cataloguing in Publication Data

Orr, Sandra, 1947-

HURON ~ Grand Bend to Southampton

Includes bibliographical references.
ISBN 1-55046-059-5

1. Huron, Lake, Region (Mich. and Ont.) – Guidebooks.
1. Title.

FC3095.H87077   1993   917.13'2   C93-093610-8
F1059.HH95077   1993

Design and Typography by Daniel Crack,
Kinetics Design & Illustration
Printed in Canada

First published in 1993 by
Stoddart Publishing Co. Limited
34 Lesmill Road
Toronto, Canada   M3B 2T6
(416) 445-3333

A BOSTON MILLS PRESS BOOK
The Boston Mills Press
132 Main Street
Erin, Ontario   N0B 1T0

The publisher gratefully acknowledges the support of
the Canada Council, Ontario Ministry of Culture and
Communications, Ontario Arts Council and Ontario
Publishing Centre in the development of writing and
publishing in Canada.

Contents

Ravelle General Store, Grand Bend, c. 1920
– Courtesy of the Lambton Heritage Museum

Preceding pages 2 &3
A day at Grand Bend's beach, 1930. Grand Bend's
beaches continue to be popular today.
– Courtesy of the Lambton Heritage Museum

Receiving the monarch at Kincardine Harbour, c. 1890. Range lights were used on the pier and the lighthouse during stormy weather. The schooner Sligo is docked, waiting for cargo to be loaded.

– COURTESY OF THE
KINCARDINE LACAC

Acknowledgments

PHOTOGRAPHS AND INFORMATION IN THIS BOOK were recovered from many sources. These include local newspapers on microfilm, as well as journals and record books.

Photographs of Grand Bend and its surrounding area were borrowed from the Lambton Heritage Museum. According to registrar Paul Miller, the museum has been actively collecting photographs for about four years. Some of these photographs were used in a book that Miller compiled with director-curator Bob Tremain, called *Grand Bend: Images of Yesteryear*. A number of the images that appear in this book were retrieved as postcards from the Amos General Store, Grand Bend, when it went out of business. Many of the photographs are the work of local photographer Joseph Senior, from Exeter.

Nap Cantin of St. Joseph has built an archives in a small building behind his house in order to preserve photos and newspaper clippings concerning his grandfather, Narcisse Cantin. Sometimes referred to as the "Father of the Seaway," Narcisse Cantin had ambitious plans for St. Joseph.

In Bayfield, Margaret MacLeod Fawcett has kept a scrapbook full of photos and clippings about her fisherman father, Louie MacLeod. She has lent these to the Bayfield Archives. Louie's story was previously included in Fred Landon's book, *Lake Huron*. His boat, the *Helen MacLeod II*, a Huron boat, was restored and displayed for a time in the Museum of Great Lakes History in Detroit under the name *Anna S. Piggott*.

Ray Scotchmer, assistant curator, and Claus Breede, director-curator, at the Huron County Museum in Goderich have been collecting photographs by the Goderich-based photographer R.R. Sallows for about the past five years. Some of the work chosen for this book was donated by a family member from Georgia, U.S.A. These photographs are previously unpublished. Al Falconer, senior technician at the Huron County Museum, made reproductions of photographs donated to the museum by local residents.

The LACAC (Local Architectural Conservation Advisory Committee) in Kincardine, with chairperson Vern Fry and member Brian Bailey, has made copies of photographs from about 500 glass negatives taken by local photographer J.H. Scougall. The collection belongs to Nancy Lambert and is in the process of being donated to the Bruce County Museum.

Curator Barbara Ribey and staff of the Bruce County Museum have collected and made copies of original photographs of scenes from Port Elgin and Southampton, among other communities.

The author is grateful to any others who lent photographs or supplied information for this book. These include Ethel Poth, Harry Baker, Mabel Middleton, Eugene C. McGee, Barbara Hawkins, Teresa Courtney, Captain Robert Wilson, Ron Pennington, Lloyd Atfield, Harold Bettger, Bernadine Kinney, Blaise Ducharme, Jim Sherratt, Ken Chisholm, Phil Gemeinhardt, Jean Muldoon, Cecil Pollock, Aileen Ravelle, Olive Webb, Mac Campbell, and John and Mary Wain.

Information and photographs were also obtained from the National Archives in Ottawa, the Ontario Archives in Toronto, and the Regional Room at the University of Western Ontario, London.

The encouragement of the Ontario Arts Council in the research and writing of this book is sincerely appreciated. I also thank the many others who have helped in various ways to make this book possible.

I would like to thank my family for their love and support, with special thanks to Angela and Gentry.

An artist painting on the Bayfield River provides a moment of reflection for local residents, c. 1947.

Evening at Southampton
— Belden Atlas 1880

Chapter One

Survey and Early Settlement
of the Coastline

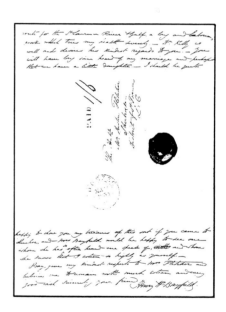

*A letter from the papers of
Henry Wolsey Bayfield.*

– COURTESY OF ONTARIO ARCHIVES

YEARS AGO, YOU COULD WALK ALONG THE CANADIAN SHORES OF LAKE HURON, smell the air, skim a pebble across the water and, unless you were in one of the small ports along the lake, chances are you wouldn't see a schooner, a scow or a fishing tug anywhere.

Today, there is a seemingly endless row of cottages, often two or three deep, along the shore. There may be a few blackened spots from campfires, a few hulks of wrecks such as the *Malta*, destroyed at Bayfield in the late 1880s, but except during the summer season, the beach is deserted.

Before present-day Lake Huron was formed, there existed a post-glacial lake called Lake Algonquin. Lake Huron's eastern shore is marked by an inland bluff that extends from Goderich to the south end of the Pinery. The bluff and other demarcations were created after the retreat of a glacial sheet that also left inland hills of gravel and sandy loam.

Underwater divers have found submerged trees just south of Bayfield. Fossils from the Devonian era, roughly 395-345 million years ago, have been found in beach pebbles. Sites once occupied by of the fluted-point people, game hunters, have been found along the ancient shores of Lake Huron, with some finds dating as early as 10,000 B.C.

It wasn't until much later that Lake Huron became the "freshwater sea" that Champlain referred to in his journals. The coastal area was populated by Huron tribes until epidemic diseases and Iroquois raids decimated the Huron as a nation in the mid-1600s. However, surviving bands of Hurons continued to trade goods with the Hudson's Bay Company well into the 19th century.

Fur traders worked the more northerly section of the shore. In addition to trapping, they traded with the Chippewa at the Saugeen for fish, corn, venison and maple sugar, which they later shipped to Detroit.

The few settlers who arrived during the late 1820s and early 1830s discovered an inhospitable wilderness. They settled along the rivers and streams that flow into the lake, so as to be near cheap transportation.

Neither the fur traders nor the Hudson's Bay Company encouraged settlement, but the area was populated in slowly increasing numbers in spite of objections by the traders.

To the first survey ships that arrived, the shore must have appeared as an indistinct grey blur. Fog was one of the perils of Lake Huron, and fishermen and boaters soon learned to be aware. The mournful sound of the occasional foghorn announces a shore that often lies completely hidden.

Captain Gother Mann, explorer and member of the British Admiralty, described the Canadian shore as a "great solitude" when he looked for defence sites in 1788. Lake Huron remained largely unexplored until 1815, when Henry Wolsey Bayfield began detailed soundings of the area. Bayfield spent four years in an open boat in order to perform his survey of the lake. In winter he determined depths by chopping holes in the ice along the shore and taking soundings, a process in which weighted lines or rods are dropped into the water to measure its depth. From Bayfield's detailed soundings of the eastern shores of Lake Huron, British Admiralty charts were printed in 1822.

Bayfield and other early surveyors lived in tents in the summer and bark huts in the winter. Later, they moved into log shanties.

There is now a succession of summer resorts and settled farmland on Lake Huron's eastern shores. But the early years of settlement were a struggle. There was virtually no clearing until Goderich was started, until Brewster had a mill, or until the London road was built. Even after that, clearing was slow for decades.

Many farmers gave up the struggle to clear their wilderness farms and went to work on the roads instead. Lake Huron settlers were cited for their lack of initiative and enterprise when compared to settlers in Chicago and Detroit. But their difficulties were

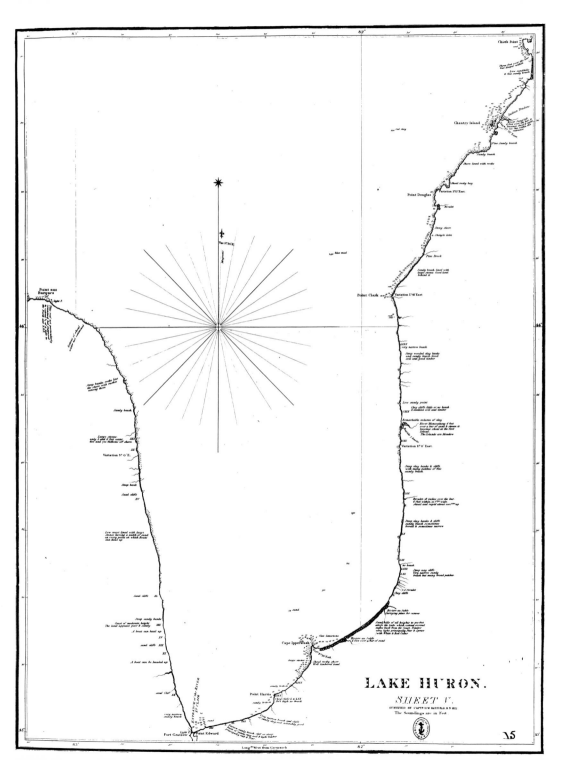

Survey map by Henry Wolsey Bayfield, 1822.

– COURTESY OF THE NATIONAL ARCHIVES OF CANADA

caused more by the geography of the area than anything else. The mouths of the small rivers were difficult to approach because of shoals, rocks, and the prevailing westerly winds that would drive a ship aground. Between Douglas Point and Southampton, areas to be avoided by ship included Lacombe Bank, Welsh Bank, Scougall Bank, and Belcher Reef. The reef around Chantry Island was especially infamous for claiming ships.

For many years, canoes were the only watercraft seen on the lake, with the odd cruising warship. Then came the sailing schooners, which gave way to steamers, and eventually to lake freighters.

Lake Huron teemed with fish. As a result, many French families, with names such as Gelinas, Ducharme, Denomme and Bedard, settled here in the late 1830s to escape hard times in Quebec due to crop failures and reduced prices. Some of the area's families' roots extend to French Canada in the mid-17th century. The French fishermen settled on thin 25-acre plots of land along the lakefront. Life was not easy for the French community during early settlement. They eked out their living by selling catches of white-

14

fish and herring to Detroit. They were charged with theft by the Canada Company when they cut timber from company land.

The Canada Company was a land-speculation firm founded in England. It bought a huge tract of land near Lake Huron, called the Huron Tract, from the British government. This land was later sold to settlers. Originally, the company promised to provide roads and other services to the region. However, problems arose when the company failed to amass the capital that it had anticipated. As a result, the settlers had to fend for themselves. Among the Canada Company's founding members were Dr. William Dunlop, Anthony Van Egmond, and John Galt, each of whom were to become key players in the region's development.

By the mid-19th century, settlement was in full swing. Lumbering, shipbuilding and fishing enterprises were started on the region's numerous rivers. Harbours were built and maintained with difficulty owing to continuous silting and damage from spring run-off.

In 1826, at the mouth of the Menesetung River (now called the Maitland River), W.F. Gooding established a trading post. It was here that the town of Goderich was born. The original town plan included eight streets radiating from a central park or square. In 1841, an octagonal jail with a courtyard was constructed. A chapel and governor's house were built later. A courthouse was built in Market Square in 1854.

The celebrated octagonal plan for Goderich was designed by John Galt. Fred Landon wrote that "the visitor to Goderich today who finds himself lost can blame this Scottish novelist who decided that around a central park the streets should radiate like the spokes of a wheel. Many an automobile driver makes the circle of the hub at least twice before finding the proper outlet." Today, there are signs on the corners that indicate which businesses are on a particular street. Even so, locals often find it necessary to make the circle more than once, and some residents of 40 years have ceased giving directions.

As a port, Goderich had an inauspicious start. With a rotting wharf, no ships, and a few scattered, mean wooden houses, its growth was slow and painful. It is now the most important port on the eastern shore of Lake Huron. It is the only really safe, deep harbour, with soundings of 19-20 feet and a main channel protected by a breakwall.

In spite of well-laid plans, Goderich remained in a backward state for quite some time. Efforts were constantly made to bring in more settlers. Dr. William Dunlop, Goderich's indefatigable citizen, described the ports in glowing terms for the Canada Company, but

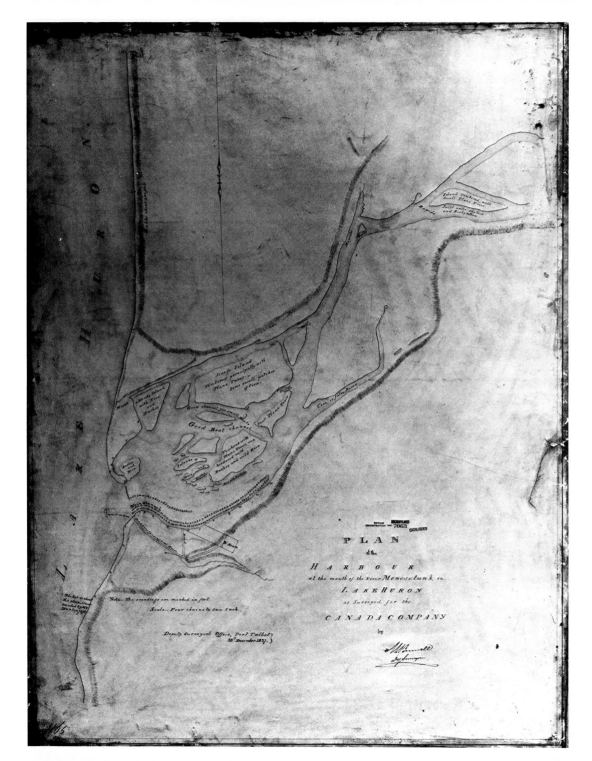

The mouth of the
Menesetung River, 1827.
– COURTESY OF THE
ONTARIO ARCHIVES

A Port Elgin pioneer farm, c. 1860.

difficulties with roads, bridges, harbours and services such as schools and churches lasted decades. It was with irony that visitors to the area noticed the town's great plans on paper while in sparse clearings most of its edifices were scarcely better than shanties.

The original map of Southampton was laid out by Robert Lynn in 1851. Provisions were made for a courthouse, jail, public offices, music hall, etc., with hopes that the town would become a great port like its namesake in England. For many years Southampton on the Saugeen was a fishing centre, with three hotels, blacksmiths, a bell founder and many cows. In 1854, a land sale in Southampton was attended by 10,000 people. The town was so overcrowded that the men had to sleep in the bush, snatching bread half-cooked from the baker who worked day and night. Provisions had to be brought in from Owen Sound. Dollars came into the office of the Crown land's agent so fast that he did not have time to count them, but threw them into a large clothes basket.

In a 1851 letter to his family, William Fraser, an early pioneer, described the town of Kincardine. There were five merchants, three taverns, two sawmills, several other houses, and work had just begun on a chapel. "I feel a little amused," he wrote, "when I hear continually of Queen's Street, Princess Street, Albert Street, Park Street, whilst only a few houses are seen at a time."

In those days, sailing schooners and scows ran every other day from Kincardine to

Philip Cress.

Henry Zinkan

Isaac E. Bowman

TANNERY & RESIDENCES OF **ZINKAN, CRESS & Co**, PORT ELGIN, ONTARIO
MANUFACTURERS OF SPANISH SOLE LEATHER

Goderich for 3 York shillings. An eagerly awaited steamboat was expected to replace them any day. That day finally came in 1832, when the Canada Company, so remiss in many of its other services, built a steamboat to run between ports on Lake Huron and Lake Erie.

Port Elgin's settlement began along one main street, Market Street. A mill and a tavern located at a crossroads formed the basis for this fast-growing industrial community. Mill Creek was easier to dam than the Saugeen and thus lent itself early to settlers' enterprise. Farm lots were re-surveyed and designated as village lots.

However, for most places on Lake Huron's Canadian shore, rapid growth was the exception rather than the rule. Maps were drawn for towns and cities that never developed. Railways, power companies and canals were proposed time and again. Pamphlets and maps were printed, but the plans never got off the ground.

Other towns did not grow as expected. They were obsessed by their smallness. For example, Tiverton was to become a town when the projected electric railway came through, but the railway did not materialize. Quite often, the hamlets or towns died slow deaths when the main railway passed them by a few miles.

The story of Lake Huron's eastern coast is one of hope and isolation, of a feeling of separation from Toronto, London and other major centres. But at least the lake and the beach were there. And if the early settlers could not sell their goods to the major centres, eventually tourists from the major centres would come to them.

PRECEDING PAGE

**The Zinkan Tannery,
Port Elgin, c. 1880.**
    – COURTESY OF THE
        BELDEN ATLAS 1880

Mr. and Mrs. Southcott, Grand Bend pioneers

Chapter Two

Settlement

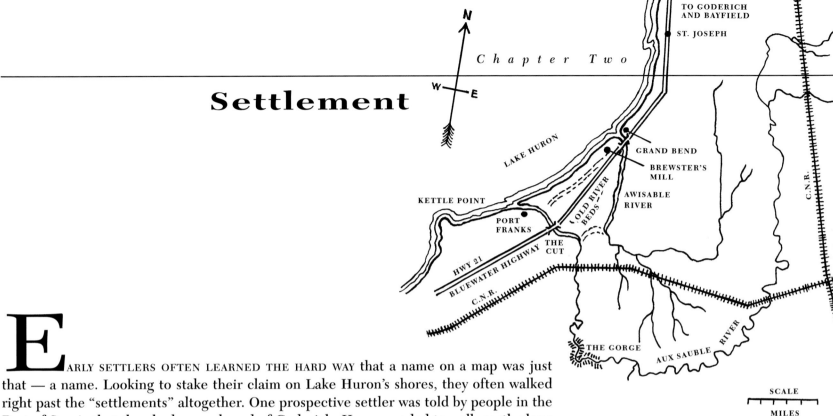

Map of Grand Bend,
Port Franks,
and Brewster's Mill.

ARLY SETTLERS OFTEN LEARNED THE HARD WAY that a name on a map was just that — a name. Looking to stake their claim on Lake Huron's shores, they often walked right past the "settlements" altogether. One prospective settler was told by people in the Port of Sarnia that they had never heard of Goderich. He proceeded to walk north along the lake anyway, thinking he might find some isolated cabin where the host would invite him to stay for a week. It was like that in the early 1800s: There was the odd dwelling, but little progress had been made in the way of settlement.

Before the Bayfield mill was built in the 1850s, settlers had to walk from Grand Bend to Goderich to take advantage of the grist mill. The grinding of flour took so long that settlers often had to wait for days. Compounding the problem, the mill had difficulty finding headwater in the summer, was washed out in the spring and frozen over in the winter.

The few stores that existed in Grand Bend in those days were housed in small board or log shanties. They served two or three customers a day, who came at all hours. The same was true for early post offices in the region.

Building Grand Bend's Centre Street also presented problems. Clearing the trees was difficult enough, but the fallen timber lay in giant heaps for months. The remaining

Mustard's sawmill, Bayfield, c. 1918. Saw- and grist mills provided essential services for the settlers.
– Courtesy of Ethel Jowett Poth

stumps created hazards for the stages and wagons. Buildings were scattered and primitive-looking.

Even as late as 1875, visitors were not impressed. Allan Duncan, a Wyoming, Ontario, farmer, wrote that while there was a considerable amount of fishing going on in Lake Huron, Grand Bend was thoroughly uninviting with its three taverns, two stores and a mill. When he reached Bayfield, he described it as a "miserable and decayed-looking village. The inhabitants are very jubilant that the government is spending $50,000 on their harbour, but my opinion is that they will never make a harbour of it." He was obviously glad to get home.

Duncan was not alone in his opinions. Many strangers thought the idea of building ports and harbours perfectly absurd because of the northwest gales and the heavy silting

Bayfield Bridge, 1879

– BELDEN ATLAS 1879

Southampton train station, c. 1907

across the river mouths. Nevertheless, the settlers came. They floated down rivers on rafts loaded with all their worldly possessions — chickens, cows, stoves — to start life in a new community.

The settlers' optimism for their communities' future was evident in the elaborate plans that they laid for their towns. There were to be many streets with grand names, and provisions were made for municipal buildings, graveyards and churches.

Nowhere was this optimism more evident than in Kincardine. Each of Kincardine's streets was to have a bridge across the river, an impractical but marvellous idea. Unlike Grand Bend and its surrounding area, Kincardine was almost entirely free of swamps. Within the town, there was beech, maple, elm, hemlock and a few oak. Kincardine's first settlers were Allan Cameron, who kept a hotel, and William Withers, who had a sawmill.

Early settlers in the Bruce had to get their supplies from Kincardine, and as a result, early storekeepers there were many and prosperous. The stores were spread out because there was uncertainty for years about where the town's centre would be.

Kincardine's first mills were made of logs and were of modest dimensions. Footpaths between trees and stumps were the only routes from one dwelling to another or down to the lake. Animals would wander at will. The steamer *Ploughboy* arrived regularly and a scow was rowed out to her if the weather was fine, which it often was not.

A surveyor could obtain time by placing a mark on a stump. Such stumps were angled in sundial fashion and affixed with metal pointing tools in their centres. When the sun was up, a shadow was created, and the time of day could be determined.

In winter the area a town serviced depended on sleighing conditions. Winter was the best time of year to travel if the snow was hard and packed.

The first survey of Southampton was made in 1851 — a town plot at the mouth of the Saugeen River. Captains John Spence and William Kennedy arrived to begin fishing ventures. They were followed by James Orr, who opened a tavern. The first winter was marked by privation, as a boat from Goderich, laden with supplies, went down in a gale. All aboard perished. For the settlers who did not move to other settlements for the winter, supplies had to be brought in from Owen Sound through forests and deep snow.

Southampton was laid out to be a large town with wide streets and a harbour at the river's mouth. In the first season, it had 30 or so houses, some of them frame. Newcomers could expect weekly mail and the services of three stores. Reserves had been marked off for public buildings, churches, schools and market buildings. After the post office was established, Southampton was made a port of entry for the collection of customs. In 1855, the financially-strapped settlement imported ten times the amount of goods it exported — roughly $6,600 worth — for which it paid about $850 in duty. There are many stories about whiskey being smuggled in from the U.S. and the tricks played to elude the customs officers.

Some settlers felt the grandness of Southampton's plan was a drawback. Because of the size of its large plots, its few inhabitants, and the relative high price of land, Southampton was very slow to develop. As well, there were few farmers in the immediate area who had cleared land and who would thus need services.

By contrast, nearby Port Elgin developed much more quickly. It had the benefit of a dam and sawmill across Mill Creek. A grist mill erected in 1855 proved to be a huge convenience for the settlers. The first building in Port Elgin was a shanty built by Lachlan McLean that also served as a tavern. William Kennedy bought an unfinished log house here and kept a store. Mail was brought on foot once a week to Southampton. A privately built pier was used to load and unload both passengers and goods, and the village was able to export grain as early as 1857-58. It had as many as five churches, in addition to many pioneer industries, such as a pottery and a brewery. Although Port Elgin thrived early, the later growth of the village was not nearly as rapid.

The first buildings in Bayfield were a log boarding house, for the men working on the roads and in the nearby saw- and grist mills, and a log Canada Company store to serve them. The first settlers used a native trail as their main route to the flats, and they also forded the river. The town plot had about 13 miles of roads planned around a square, and a wide main street at a 46-degree angle to the lakeshore.

Bayfield's earliest roads, with corduroy or log surfaces, stumps and bottomless holes, were more of an obstacle course than anything else. For that reason, the lake and rivers long remained the primary transportation routes.

Small backwoods villages like Port Elgin had chartered banks so that settlers could buy land. They enjoyed their most prosperous period in the few decades after the railway came to Goderich in 1858, and to the smaller towns of Kincardine and Port Elgin in 1873.

An Old Boys' parade at Victoria Park, c. 1907.

MAP OF

SAUGEEN

TOWNSHIP

N. PART
OF SOUTHAMPTON

THE LAKE
HURON
SHORELINE

PROPOSED WIARTON
BRANCH

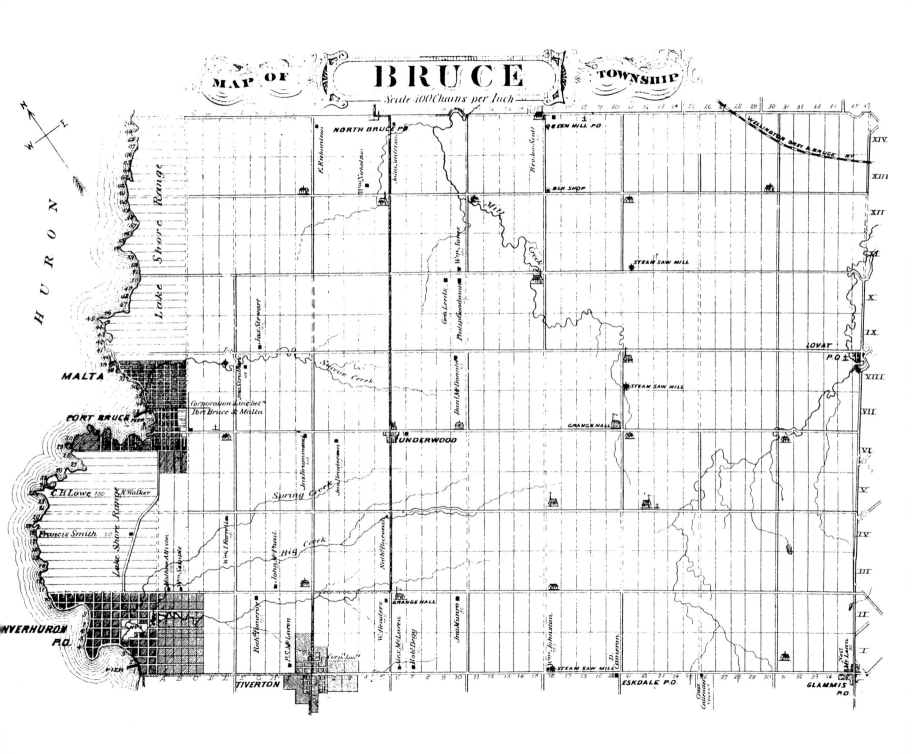

MAP OF **BRUCE** TOWNSHIP

Scale 100 Chains per Inch

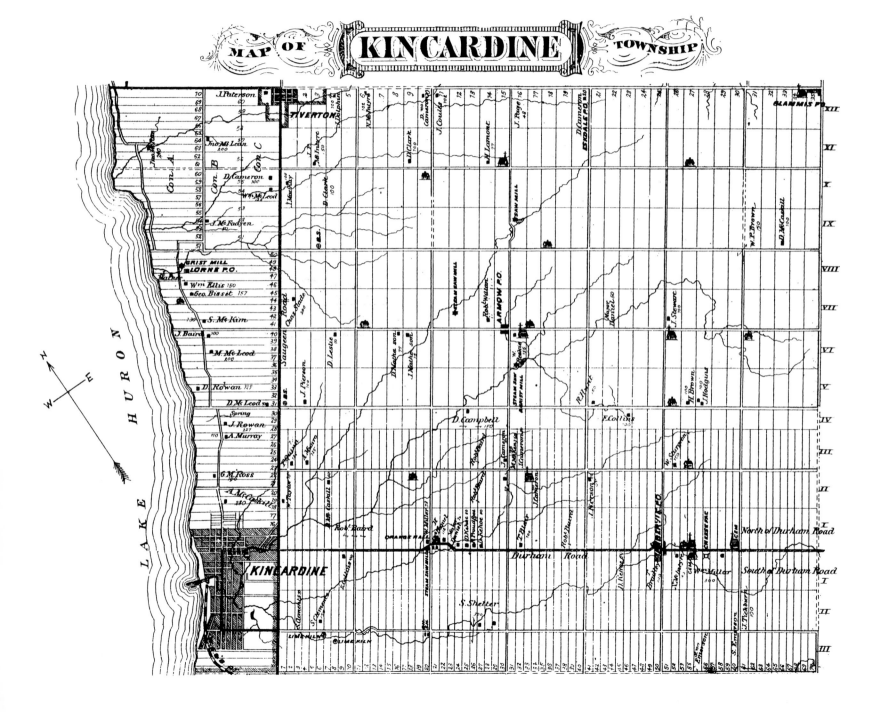

MAP OF KINCARDINE TOWNSHIP

LAKE HURON

KINCARDINE

TIVERTON

LORNE P.O.

GRIST MILL

ARNOW P.O.

GLAMMIS P.O.

EKDALE P.O.

North of Durham Road

Durham Road

South of Durham Road

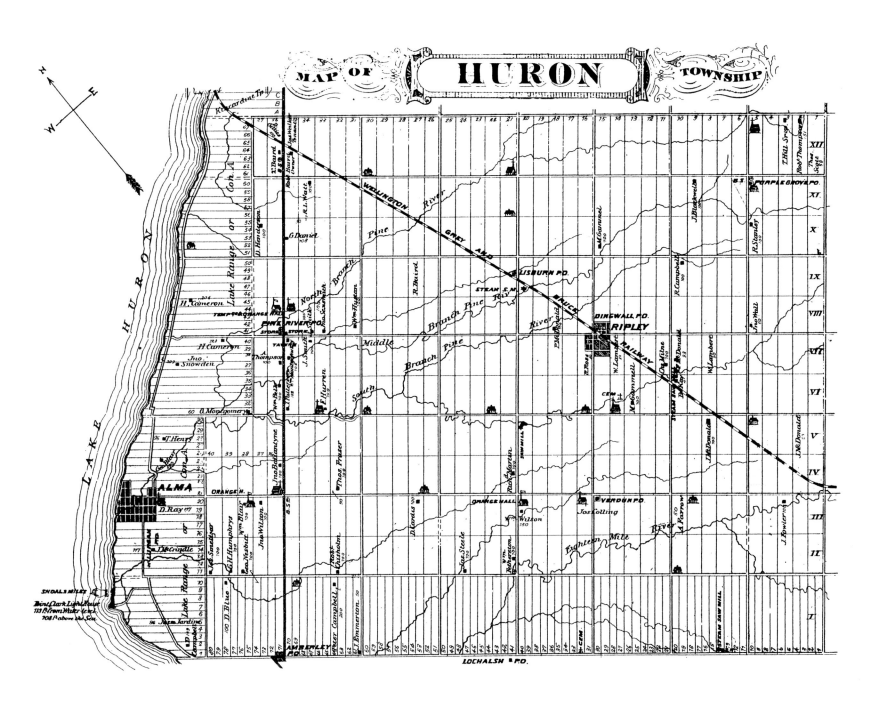

MAP OF HURON TOWNSHIP

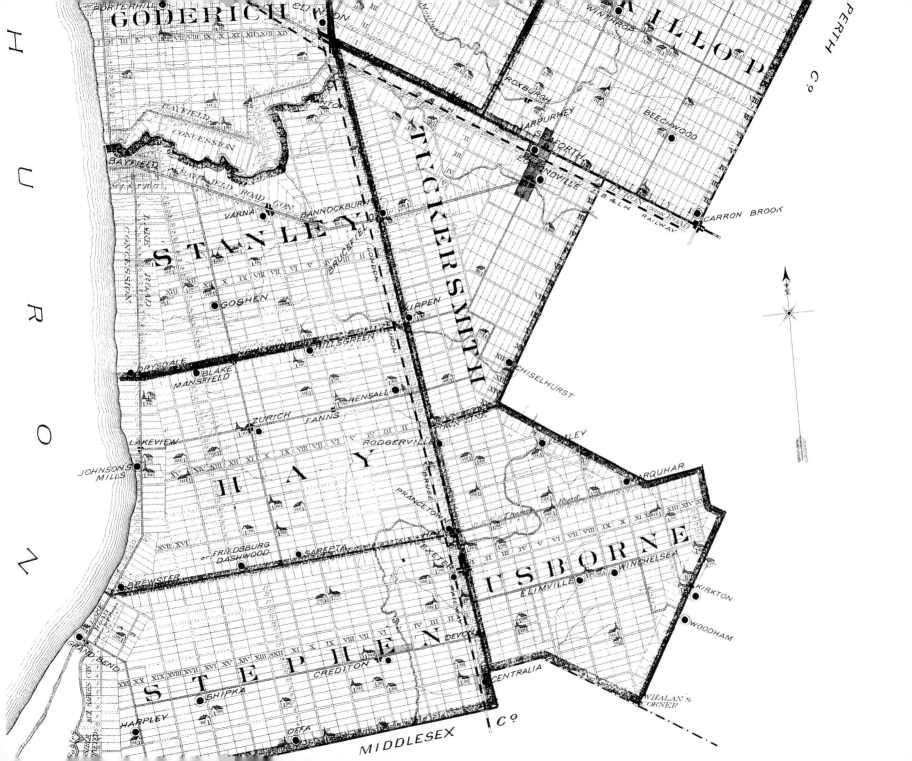

Blacksmith's shop, 1917

Chapter Three

Early Commerce

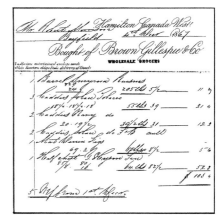

A bill from Brown, Gillespie & Co. to Morrison and Edwards, Bayfield merchants, 1867.

– COURTESY OF
UWO REGIONAL ROOM

FOR THE FRONTIER SETTLERS, RESOURCEFULNESS AND CO-OPERATION WERE the two keys to survival in their new environment. Success or failure depended as much on what they could do for each other as what they might accomplish themselves. Lake Huron's earliest commerce involved the trading of goods between ports. Schooners and steamers used to accomplish this before the railways arrived.

Sawmills were an economic priority in the fledgling settlements. In 1832, Brewster and Company bought the land and power privileges for a mill near present-day Grand Bend. According to a historical feature in a May 1938 issue of the London *Free Press*, the mill employed up to 300 hands. But the mill dam backed up the river and flooded township lands, so the mill and its owners became unpopular. The Canada Company initiated legal proceedings to obtain payment for damage due to flooding. Later, a vigilance committee destroyed the mill and dam.

By 1870, although much of the land had been purchased and some of it cleared, Grand Bend was really more of a fishing base than an agricultural settlement. But the Bend did have large peach and apple orchards. There were also mills for planing and for making shingles and moulding. There were flour and feed mills, a general store, two hotels and a daily stagecoach to Parkhill.

The early days of commerce were difficult ones. Many settlers experienced financial problems. In the Huron *Signal*, in the fall of 1854, there appeared a great list of arrears in taxes. The next year there were many, many ads for the sheriff's sale of lands. The economic success of one community often came at the expense of another. For example, when William Sutton built Kincardine's first grist mill settlers no longer had to travel to Port Albert to grind their wheat. Not only did Port Albert's mill suffer, so did the economy of the whole town. Early Port Albert residents had high hopes for their town, but prosperity never materialized. Streets and buildings were planned but never built.

During the 1860s, Bayfield was a mecca of commerce, handling grain and lumber at its port. Wagonmakers, blacksmiths, coopers, saddlers, and carriagemakers established themselves as well. Dressmakers, tailors and shoemakers were also common. The general store carried everything, including shoes and hats and ladies' red gaiters.

Blacksmiths at work in Southampton, c. 1875.
– COURTESY OF
BRUCE COUNTY MUSEUM

Hauling in the fish catch in handmade barrels. An important industry to the region, fish was packaged and transported on ice in a wide variety of barrels.
– Courtesy of the
Bruce County Museum

The trade out of Goderich in 1853 was primarily flour and fish. Goderich was not yet the major port it was to become. At Goderich in January 1853, the market prices of goods were as follows: Flour cost 15 shillings to 16 shillings 3 pence per bushel; fall wheat was 2 shillings 9 pence to 3 shillings per bushel; spring wheat, 2 shillings 6 pence per 34 pounds; and pork 4 and a quarter to 5 dollars per hundred; butter, 10 pence to 80 pence per pound. Herring was the chief catch, with about 2,500 barrels per season. Fish was sold on ice, by the barrel, half barrel, hogshead, puncheon, quarter cask, box basket or wagon load. (A hogshead was a large cask holding 63-140 gallons; a puncheon held 70-120 gallons.)

Trim little schooners, such the ones built by John and Robert Rowan in Kincardine, plied the waters between Goderich and Kincardine. A June 1854 issue of the Huron *Signal* considered these schooners as evidence of a very forward state "of the new country to the north."

Unloading maple sap for sugar and syrup.

In 1854, Goderich could boast of an axe factory and some houses of a substantial character, but the town lamented the state of its harbour, with rotting and broken planks on its wharves. Goderich looked with envious eyes to Kincardine and its neat little boats that sailed between the two ports and to Toronto with stoves, clocks, buffalo rugs and pianos. The town felt neglected and stunted in its growth, and so discussed plans and debentures for railways from Toronto or London to Goderich.

The rivalry between Goderich and other communities was bitter. In November 1853, a Kincardine-built boat was wrecked while trying to make the Goderich harbour during a northwest gale. The Guelph *Herald* made the remark that since "it is a very difficult harbour to make at all times, she was dashed against the north pier." In response, the Huron *Signal* defended its harbour, saying, "The entrance and approach is now free of rocks and shoals for miles," and pointed the blame at the captain and the seaworthiness of his ship. A northwest blow was always a matter of concern when trying to make port.

In 1867, Kincardine was a prospering community with general stores, hotels, foundries, wool factories, tanneries, pearl ash factories, and fishing enterprises. Exports such as salt, wheat, barley, peas, grass seed, flour, butter, pearl ash, wool, pork and tanbark reflected the fruits of the farming hinterland.

The completion of the Buffalo-Brantford-Goderich railway line, part of the Grand Trunk Railway, was eagerly anticipated by all the ports along Lake Huron. Completed in 1858, it opened up other markets to the enterprising settlers. However, the main line was often snowbound, and the through train to Kincardine would be held up for days. The wood-burning locomotive would jerk along and jolt as the lead wheels struck the end of each rail. The train occasionally stopped and backed up a mile if it missed a passenger.

Toll gates controlled the traffic on the roads to some extent and were looked after by big men who could enforce the tolls. To get into Goderich in the 1870s, the tolls in the table at right applied.

In the early days of commerce, farmers would bring their produce and livestock to town. Pigs would be weighed at the town hall and then taken to the pork factory. Cattle would be run through the streets. Milk and cream were brought to the town creamery in wagons. Early newspapers were full of advertisements for stray animals. If one forgot to shut the gate at night, in the morning a cow or goat would be in the garden, eating the nasturtiums and the vegetables. The strays might run around the garden a few times before escaping back through the gate.

GODERICH TOLLS
~ 1870 ~

DOUBLE TEAM, HORSE OR OXEN
10¢, 15 ¢ return

TEAM	5 ¢
MAN ON HORSEBACK	1 ¢
MAN ON FOOT	*free*
FUNERALS	*free*
WEDDINGS	*free*

In the 1850s, the trading post at Southampton sold fish and maple sugar to Detroit. As many as 130 houses had already been built. The groundwork had been laid for the great port that it was to become.

However, the town grew gradually, primarily attracting settlers to the lucrative trade in fish and furs. The first manufacturing industry in Southampton was a steam-powered sawmill. A grist mill, distillery and woollen mill soon followed. Such factories existed in the small towns to serve the immediate needs of the settler and the farmer. When these factories were no longer needed, or the goods could be produced more efficiently in the larger centres, they disappeared.

By the 1870s, at the peak of the lake shipping era, farmers could ship their products to the major centres for processing. Schooners could regularly be seen in ports such as Southampton and Port Elgin. Farmers lined up along the waterfront with their wagons full of grain. Hardwood logs and lumber were shipped by raft or steamer.

Liquor was the scourge of the fledgling communities. Temperance festivals were held, and the women were given "great credit for their exertions." However, if the schedule of convictions for Huron and Bruce counties in November of 1853 is any indication, they were not too successful.

Similar convictions were common for the next few years and attest to the rough times that everyone endured. The list did not exclude businessmen and prominent people either. For instance, Christopher Crabb, a Goderich entrepreneur, was charged by the Queen for larceny, and by Richard Stanbury twice for assault. Crabb was a merchant who sold dry goods, hardware and salt, in addition to 500 barrels of "*PURE UNADULTERATED*" whisky, in 1853.

By 1860, the list of convictions was four times larger than 1853, comprising 13 full pages of foolscap for Huron and Bruce. The magistrate's handwriting was hard to read. A clerk complained that "they might as well write in Gaelic. Few educated men could translate these for $1.00 a sheet let alone $1.00 for thirteen sheets."

The county jail in Goderich, lit by an octagonal lantern in the central stair hall, had so many visitors when it was first built that it was subsequently closed to the public for 130 years. There were apparently several executions in the jail, one of which was the hanging of Edward Jardine for the murder of Lizzie Anderson. Jardine apparently threw his girlfriend down a well. Most of the inmates of the jail were drunks, the homeless, or

N O V E M B E R

~ 1 8 5 3 ~

C O N V I C T I O N S

ALL MORE OR LESS
THE RESULT OF DRINK

23 ASSAULTS

1 DOGGING HOGS

2 TRESPASSES

1 ROBBING GARDEN

3 MISDEMEANOURS

1 ARRESTING CATTLE

3 MALICIOUS INJURIES

1 DRUNKENNESS

Duck hunting, 1909

the mentally ill. Beds were wooden cots, each with a grey blanket. Breakfast was porridge and molasses. As additional punishment, prisoners received only bread and water. Bills were sent to the county for the inmates' needs.

Many storekeepers solved the shoplifting problems their own way. One Bayfield storekeeper caught a man who had stolen butter and hidden it under his hat. He backed the thief up against the stove and held him there until the butter ran down his head. Butter could be traded for merchandise, such as lamps.

During the 19th century, residents of the rural area along the shores was known for their drunkenness. The many hotels and taverns situated every few miles did good business. In fact, taverns and distilleries were often the first establishments in any settlement. Each port had many hotels, and if at first they were merely log shanties they were soon replaced by many-storeyed brick structures. Sixty-one new liquor licences were granted to establish in Huron in 1894. Two more would have been granted if their premises hadn't burned down. In these tough frontier times, men would stop stages at the bottom of a hill, or simply rob passengers on foot, and then gallop away with their loot. Hotels were continually robbed. Since there were many taverns along the roads, no man had to travel far without drink. Quite often the drink in another town tasted better than that at home, hence the great number of patrons who arrived and departed on horseback. Gavin Green wrote about these wild men in *The Old Log School*. They were giants who stopped at all watering holes. They would sometimes clear out the barrooms, throwing everything into the street.

A Goderich jailer and family, c. 1900. Drunkenness and crime went hand in hand at the early settlements. Early jails were guarded by huge men like Patrick O'Loughlin (left).

Chantry Island lighthouse, c. 1895

Chapter Four

Lighthouses

Lighthouses along the eastern shores of Lake Huron guide seamen through often treacherous waters. The lighthouses are all different: tall, short, squat, graceful, square, or tapered. Some were built as early as 1859 in response to the continual wrecks and loss of life.

In the early years, navigation through wind, rocks and shoals was always difficult, but especially so during a northwest gale. There were many wrecks and many lives lost when ships attempted to enter eastern Lake Huron ports during a blow. These wrecks, dozens for some ports, often occurred within sight of land, on the approach to a harbour's mouth, or on the beaches. Schooners and brigs went down most frequently but steamers fared little better in the storms. Bodies and personal belongings routinely washed up on shore. Bills for the burial of unidentified people were presented to the local municipalities. When entire ships' cargoes were lost, settlers sometimes faced starvation.

Sidewheelers (steam-powered vessels with side-paddles) such as the *Kaloolah* and the *Ploughboy* were placed in regular service in the coastal trade.

The lake and connecting waterways were lifelines for the settlements. Before roads were developed and the railway completed, schooners carried lumber and other goods between the ports. Steamers carried coal, passengers and mail.

An advertisement for an early coastal steamer, 1867.

– From *Roots & Branches of the Saugeen*, 1984, Owen Sound

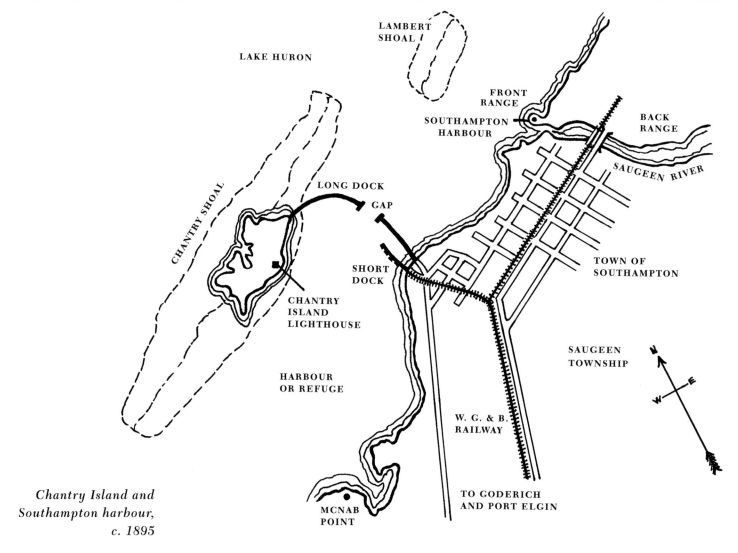

LAKE HURON

LAMBERT
SHOAL

FRONT
RANGE

SOUTHAMPTON
HARBOUR

BACK
RANGE

SAUGEEN RIVER

CHANTRY SHOAL

LONG DOCK

GAP

CHANTRY
ISLAND
LIGHTHOUSE

SHORT
DOCK

TOWN OF
SOUTHAMPTON

HARBOUR
OR REFUGE

SAUGEEN
TOWNSHIP

W. G. & B.
RAILWAY

MCNAB
POINT

TO GODERICH
AND PORT ELGIN

N

E

W

*Chantry Island and
Southampton harbour,
c. 1895*

The coastal communities made efforts to improve navigational aids and harbour facilities. They pressured the government for improvements. Channels were cut and repaired in response to accidents and storm damage. During the late 1850s, lighthouses were built to warn seamen of shoals and reefs.

In 1859, lighthouses were erected at Chantry Island and Point Clark. Their elegant towers were tall, tapered structures of graceful proportions. The towers were originally surrounded by houses, outbuildings, sheds and wharves. The first lanterns were fueled by whale oil and had open flames. Later lamps were enclosed and petroleum-oil lights were used.

At Point Clark, there is a very tall tower to warn of the reefs about 2 miles offshore. The Point Clark lighthouse is 9 storeys high, leading to the lantern. Its walls are tapered, 5 feet thick at the bottom and 2 feet thick at the top. The stone used to build the thick walls was brought from Kingston and Inverhuron. There are eight stairways with iron railings winding up to the light. The first lightkeeper, John Young, and his wife lived in a small stone cottage near the lighthouse from 1873. Saw- and grist mills, stores and other buildings were soon erected near the lighthouse, but the community did not develop. Some buildings were moved elsewhere to become farm homes. The Point Clark lighthouse became a museum in 1970 and retains its original lantern.

Another majestic tower was built from 1859 to 1862 on Chantry Island to warn of the reefs surrounding the island. The Chantry Island lighthouse, situated about one-half mile from the mainland town of Southampton, is very similar to the Point Clark lighthouse. Its dioptric lens was of French manufacture and had a range of 15 miles. It has now been replaced with an automatic light. The lighthouse keeper's stone house had a fireplace in the south wall, a slate roof, and rooms on each side of the main hall. The tower has curved benches around the walls. The first lightkeeper was Captain McGregor Lambert. Upon his death, the post was given to his son, William. On many occasions, the family made heroic efforts to save the lives of people on ships wrecked on the shoals surrounding Chantry Island. In September 1879, William Lambert's son, Ross, and another crew member lost their lives when their boat capsized on the way to a boat in trouble. Chantry Island's last lighthouse keeper was Cameron Spencer, who retired in 1953. The island has now been declared a bird sanctuary.

Southampton harbour has two tapered wooden lighthouses with square lanterns. The matching pair were built in 1877, one on the end of the pier and one 100 yards upriver. There is also a lighthouse on McNab Point, south of Southampton harbour, built the same year and of identical design. It has an electric light that can be seen for about 12 miles.

Built in 1847, the Goderich lighthouse is a squat, square, 2-storey building standing on a 100-foot bluff above the harbour and flour mills. It was equipped with a mercury vapour light, which in 1896 was replaced with a more modern unit. The light remains on at all times.

Building the short dock in Southampton, c. 1875.   – Courtesy of the Bruce County Museum

The lighthouse in Kincardine's harbour is situated on a high stone foundation at the harbour's basin. It was built in 1881. It is a hexagonal structure with sloping sides and three landings with wide, straight stairs. Its lantern shows a red flashing light for one second then eclipsed for four seconds. William Kay was a keeper here, as was Thomas McGaw. Like most lighthouses, it is no longer manned. The old foghorn has been replaced with a whistle. In 1874, another wooden lighthouse was constructed at the end of the pier. It had an oil-fired lamp and a reflector. The structure has since been replaced by a steel tower with a red flashing light.

It was noted in the local papers that birds, attracted to the lighthouses' powerful lights, would sometimes circle for hours until, exhausted, they would fall to the ground and die.

During harsh storms, volunteers would man rowboats to reach wrecked schooners, bailing all the while. Sometimes they were able to save crew members before the vessels and their cargo broke up entirely. Sometimes, however, the volunteers were driven back by high seas or were drowned while trying to aid a shipwreck.

The lighthouses, built in different shapes and sizes according to the needs and topography of the ports, greatly contributed to navigational safety. The freshwater sea that often looked so placid could wreak havoc on the unwary. Although currents and the location of the shoals were generally learned by experience, the lighthouses saved countless lives. Their beacons could be seen from 15 to 25 miles away, depending on weather conditions. Many of these lighthouses are now historic landmarks and curiosities. But at the turn of the century, they were necessary for the survival of ships, cargo and crew.

Goderich harbour, c. 1870

Chapter Five

The Harbours

EVEN THOUGH ENORMOUS SUMS OF MONEY WERE SPENT on port facilities, the towns came under constant criticism for the state of their harbours. Maintenance costs, such as those for dredging silt and repairing wharves, consumed large amounts of money over long periods of time. Such expenditures were necessary because, before the roads were developed and the railway completed, the harbours were a priority. Town councils continually lobbied government for improvements. Government engineer William Kingsford was placed in charge of the inspection and repair of the area's harbours in 1875. Kingsford made recommendations to Ottawa about many of the ports on the Great Lakes.

Bayfield flourished early as a grain port. Its grain was shipped to Kingston by schooner, which then returned with bricks. But getting it down to the harbour was a task in itself. The grain was hauled by horse and wagon to the brow of the hill, then it was taken down a narrow-gauge railway with a hand-powered truck to where it was dumped into 2-storey-high bins. The grain was then swept by boys for 15 cents a day, sometimes by candlelight.

In 1874, $36,000 was spent on the Bayfield harbour. However, the townspeople were convinced that an additional $10,000 was needed to make it truly safe and convenient,

Excerpt from a letter to the Secretary of Public Works, 1875. William Kingsford was the government engineer responsible for the inspection and planning of works on Lake Huron's harbours.

– COURTESY OF THE ONTARIO ARCHIVES, KINGSFORD LETTER BOOK

An aerial view of Kincardine taken by the London Free Press in 1935.

because during snow and sleet storms, schooners continued to miss the harbour's mouth, and landed on the beach or ran aground between the rocks. The wrecks would later be stripped for their oak and fittings.

All of the harbours along the eastern coast of Lake Huron silted over and had to be dredged. Dredging was a cost that had to be borne by the municipalities every few years. It tended to be postponed due to lack of funds.

The respective ports were very sensitive to remarks made about the state of their harbours. And engineer Kingsford's remarks on the harbours could be scathing. On May 20, 1875, he wrote, "Port Elgin is one of the many harbours in Canada which has experienced the misfortune of a large sum of money uselessly expended. It is directly open and exposed to the North Westerly gales, with the consequent difficulty in loading and unloading."

Nevertheless, work on the coastal harbours continued. As late as 1935, it was reported that work on the Kincardine harbour was still progressing.

With the arrival of the steamer, the urgency to improve the harbours became even greater. Farmers needed to ship their products to market. Proper harbour facilities could make a town a centre for grain handling. Before the harbours were improved, farmers piled their sleighs high with grain and lined up for the vessels. For 25 cents an hour, men shovelled grain into 2-bushel bags that had to be hoisted onto wagons, then onto scows, and then into vessels that were anchored and waiting. When the railway was completed in 1873, Kincardine lost its advantage as a grain port.

For several years, Goderich went without contact by water with other communities. That's because its early boat, the *Menesetung*, was rammed and sunk in the harbour. W.H. Smith, in his book *Canada: Past, Present, and Future*, remarked that in 1850 Goderich's piers were in a dilapidated state. Its cribs were covered with water and it was dangerous for vessels to enter on a dark night.

Despite these difficulties, local men began to build boats. Henry Marlton established a yard on Ship Island in Goderich harbour. From 1848 to 1907, the Marltons built about 70 schooners, tugs and steamers, which delivered cargo to the eastern shores of Lake Huron and elsewhere.

But the Goderich harbour was in constant need of attention. In 1894, the harbour required repairs totalling $6,000. No action had been taken by 1896, and it was decided by town council that $18,000 was now necessary to put the harbour in proper condition. Goderich became the most important port on the eastern shore primarily due to the large sums of money that were spent on it. Eventually, piers were built to protect the harbour from the waves during gales, and breakwalls were added to the north and south to protect the harbour entrance. In the past 130 years, there have been about 40 seasons of high water levels.

Because Goderich was the largest port in the area, it was decided that the town would be linked by railway to Stratford. Despite other ports' continuous lobbying to have railway tracks linked to them, the line was completed between Goderich and Stratford in 1858. Round-trip excursions to the Muskokas were advertised around this time.

Waiting for the tug at Southampton's dock, c. 1890.
– Courtesy of the Bruce County Museum

Southampton harbour with Goderich-built tugs and scows, c. 1900.

Gathering stone for the pier at Grand Bend, c. 1900.

The record of government revenue, the "Blue Book," listed 1879 excise duties at Goderich on licences, spirits, malt, tobacco and cigars, and petroleum at 20 cents. Other major centres on the lakes pointed out that the amount of duty collected at Goderich was only a fraction of that collected at Port Huron and wondered why it would be kept open. There were complaints about the excessive cost of collecting this tiny revenue.

The harbour could be a dangerous place. At Goderich, two barrels of blasting powder were stored in a shop. They had been picked up by fishermen four or five years earlier. Two boys were smoking and threw a match into one of the barrels. They died soon after the powder exploded, setting fire to their shirtsleeves and pantaloons.

In Port Albert, in 1868, $2,200 was voted for harbour improvements. The repairs consisted of depositing gravel and clay behind the pier works.

The journey up the lake to such small ports was dangerous for small vessels because of the possibility of sudden storms. In the early days, the only warning of an approaching storm was a basket hung at a tall post at the harbour mouth.

Later, foghorns were introduced. A foghorn can be heard for quite some distance, depending on conditions. In 1914, the Marine Department installed one of the most powerful electric foghorns available in Canada at Goderich. Many steamships were wrecked not far from Goderich during the infamous 1913 storm. Had proper telegraph warning been available, it was thought that those ships would have sought refuge. Although Goderich had a reputation for being a fairweather harbour, it was the only port that could take large ships.

At Southampton, there were extensive works at Chantry Island that cost a great deal of money. They provided two piers of almost a mile in total length, one with a harbour gap in the middle. The pier from the shore to the island was the longest, about 2,200 feet with a gap. However, in a gale, a ship or schooner could not always make this gap and there were a number of wrecks at the mouth.

After the storm of 1913, a number of citizens beseeched Ottawa for a harbour for Inverhuron, in view of the lives that could possibly be saved in the future. The outbreak of World War I was blamed for Inverhuron not receiving a harbour.

At Port Elgin, prior to building their harbour in 1857, scows would row out to meet boats, transporting goods and people from ship to shore. A privately built pier, used for loading and unloading passengers and goods, encouraged grain export. But it came at a cost. By 1890, $80,000 had been spent on harbour renovations. The harbour has the advantage of not being situated at the mouth of a river, so there is no danger from spring flooding.

In 1902, $5,000 was set aside for a wharf at St. Joseph. The local townspeople foresaw it developing into a popular resort, and therefore thought they needed the facilities. Opponents of this allotment charged that it was a waste of money and questioned whether the spot was fit for a wharf. But the handsome Narcisse Cantin, an entrepreneur and well-known local figure, had cast a spell over the community. About $15,000 was spent to unload a few cargoes of lumber and to accommodate a few fishermen. Then the businesses and factories began to disappear and construction came to an abrupt halt. Today, there is no wharf at St. Joseph.

In 1870, Grand Bend was still known as Brewster. It had a post office, a store, a school, and a church in a log shanty. Grand Bend had three taverns, and it was common for landed seamen to be found drinking their health there. Despite its size, in 1892, the community felt a harbour was needed and a canal was dug from the "grand bend" of the Ausable River to the lake. A pier runs out into the lake north of the mouth of Parkhill Creek, which breaks the waves and slows silting. The Ausable flows from the Bend 13 miles southward to Lake Huron, but is separated from it by sandy dunes. The Pinery, 4,200 acres of sandy hills, is still owned by the Canada Company. In the early days, Brewster and the French settlement to the north were fishing settlements.

To the municipalities on the eastern shore of Lake Huron, the expenditure of enormous sums of money was always justified. The locals felt that their ports were their gateway to the world.

Goderich harbour, 1924

– PHOTO BY R.R. SALLOWS, COURTESY OF THE HURON COUNTY MUSEUM

The Helen MacLeod II,
1925
– COURTESY OF MARGARET
MACLEOD FAWCETT

Chapter Six

The Fishing Industry

A square-sterned Huron boat, 1931. The Huron boat's design originated in Goderich. It's short mast and well-balanced sails were thought to be the most practical for Lake Huron's unpredictable waters.

– COURTESY OF BOB WILSON

B Y THE TIME, THE SETTLERS HAD CLEARED A BIT OF LAND FOR FARMS, commercial fishing had already become an important industry for Southampton, Port Elgin, Inverhuron, Kincardine, right down to Grand Bend, and wherever else an inlet offered some protection from the elements.

The fishing fleet spent the good weather between March and November out on the lake. The locally built fishing boats left before dawn in fine weather. But sometimes by noon, gale-force winds had set in. The foremast was often the taller of the fishing boats' two masts. With mainsails and a jib, gaff and boom, they would set out for the American reef, weathering the gales that would sometimes spring up.

Scows would go out onto the lake and poles would be driven into the lake bottom to build pond nets to catch the fish. Even sturgeon would be caught this way.

The boats, constructed of oak or elm with pine planking, were built right in the ports. In Bayfield, Thomas Baird built the schooner *Stanley* for fisherman Alex McDonald. The Stanley had many owners before it was dismantled at the turn of the century.

The "Huron boat" was a square-sterned schooner, an open boat used for fishing or trade. Its short mast and well-balanced canvas sails made it ideal for heavy weather. Originating in Goderich, the Huron boat's square-sterned design was thought to make it

Captain Louie MacLeod mending nets.

– Courtesy of Margaret MacLeod Fawcett

*Viola Livermore (Lampman) and Neity Taylor (Deeves)
in a home-built boat, Bayfield River, c. 1929.*
– Courtesy of Phil Gemeinhardt

The Helen MacLeod II *re-fitted
as the* Anna S. Piggott, *c. 1950.*
– Courtesy of Margaret
MacLeod Fawcett

*Fishing houses and boats,
Bayfield, c. 1940.*
– Courtesy of Ethel
Jowett Poth

more manageable in rough waters than traditional double-ended boats. A true mackinaw schooner was sharp-sterned.

Although fishing was hard work, with long days spent pulling nets by hand, the industry was the mainstay of costal communities. In Southampton, the early fishing industry boomed. As many as 70 men were employed in 1884, using 18 boats with a capital investment of $30,000. At the turn of the century, the cost to outfit a tug was about $4,000, and a sailing boat about $500. The catch in Southampton averaged about 350 tons a season, worth about $14,000.

Hughie MacLeod was a pioneer fisherman and boatbuilder in Bayfield. His son, Louie, built the *Helen MacLeod II* in 1925, after the *Helen MacLeod I* had worn out 12 sets of sails and 2 motors. Constructed of red beech, the *Helen MacLeod II* had an overall length of 36 feet, a beam of 10 feet, and a 3 foot 6 inch draft. Louie used a piece of the shipwrecked *Malta* for good luck. In a November 1882 storm, the *Malta* crew had been unable to get the schooner into the harbour.

Hughie MacLeod's son, Louie, was a Bayfield fisherman for many years and his skills, both as a fisherman and sailor, were legendary. He could sail his square-sterned Huron boat in almost any weather. It was said that he could look at the water and the cloud formation and decide how the lake would be that day.

"Years ago, a four-pound trout would do us for supper. We would do about fifty pounds of trout in crocks for the winter. Then we would have to boil the trout to get the salt out of it," says Margaret MacLeod Fawcett. She reports that when her father, Louie, caught an eel the first time, he had it identified and told the government, but nothing was done about it. Lamprey eels prey on the fish population and spell disaster for fishermen. Often large percentages of fish catches are rejected because of the scarring that eels inflict. Loons were plentiful on the lake back then. They chased the fish, and many got caught in the nets and drowned.

In 1955, the *Helen MacLeod II* was restored and renamed the *Anna S. Piggott*. It was displayed for a time at the Museum of Great Lakes History in Detroit.

In addition to the Huron boat, larger wooden ships were also constructed at Goderich. Two-masted schooners, such as the *Annexation* built in 1849, were an average 76 feet long, 18 feet wide and had an 8-foot draft. Such schooners carried barley, coal, grain, salt, and tanbark. Many of the ships were heavily mortgaged. It was a disaster if they,

Bayfield fishermen, c. 1930: (from left to right) Captain Louie MacLeod, Rit McDoole, Herbie Sturgeon, and Charlie "Punch" Toms.

*Joe Ravelle with fishermen friends. Grand Bend fishermen,
c. 1930, postcard.*
    – COURTESY OF AILEEN RAVELLE

*An early cutter used for ice-
fishing. Ice-fishing was an
important pastime for the
early settlers, many of whom
were unemployed during
the winter.*
– COURTESY OF
ETHEL JOWETT POTH

*Pulling fishing boats
out of the ice.*
– COURTESY OF
MARGARET MacLEOD FAWCETT

their cargoes, or their crews were lost. These schooners required tugs to get in and out of the harbour.

There was heated controversy over where the Americans were allowed to fish and where the Canadians were not. Many Canadian fishermen resented the invisible line that was drawn across the lake, feeling they had been barred from fishing their rightful domain. As well, American fishermen were allowed to use gill nets that were twice as large as those of their Canadian counterparts. They argued that the regulations in force in 1894 cost the annual loss of $5 million or $6 million to the fishermen of Ontario. The Canadian government official, Mr. Wilmot, argued that Canadian fish do not migrate to American waters. Needless to say, the Canadian fishermen bitterly resented their government's position.

In the winter, fishing on the ice kept everyone busy. In Bayfield, for example, if the ice looked good and was well-anchored, holes were dug and nets were set down. With roughly half the people out of work in the winter, ice-fishing was beneficial to the villages.

But ice-fishing could be dangerous. One day, a fishing party out of Bayfield found itself in trouble when the ice broke up leaving five men and a dog afloat on ice. Men went out in a boat and rescued two of the stranded men, but when they returned, the floe had drifted away with the three remaining men. Ice prevented the rescue boat from going out again. After two days, the stranded men killed and ate their dog. Two days later, they were blown ashore at Blake, where a native found them collapsed on the beach. One man lost a hand and a foot to frostbite, but the others survived without serious injury.

The fish catch varied from year to year. The 1898 season was considered by fishermen to be the least successful of the decade. In part, this was because of the line drawn across the lake, due west from Goderich, restricting their domain. Canadian fishermen felt it caused their catch to be 30 to 40 percent below the average for the previous ten years. But cold, bitter weather also reduced the catch.

In 1894, as many as 70,700 men fished the Canadian waters of Lake Huron in 1,178 large vessels and 34,100 small boats. By the 1940s, fishing on Lake Huron involved only a handful of men. The total catch was also a fraction of what it had been. This was a far cry from pioneer days when a man could climb a tree, spot a silvery cloud in the water, and tell the fishermen, who would then encircle the school with their nets. The nets were drawn to a shore, and the fish thrown on the beach. The size of the catch was often

Fishing in a scow, 1907.

Raphael O'Loughlin on the beach with the North Star, Kingsbridge, c. 1922.
    – COURTESY OF
    BERNADINE KINNEY

limited by the number of available barrels or salt. Farmers could take two barrels of trout in a few hours. At this time, the passenger pigeons were so thick that they could be knocked down with a stick. The few people who settled on the coast dined on fish, venison, passenger pigeon, and berries.

In 1908, the fishing industry was still flourishing in Grand Bend. Fish was purchased three times a week by the A.W. Selkirk Fish Company of Port Huron, Michigan. In March 1914, in Grand Bend, 41 trout were caught in one day. Fishermen could haul in sturgeon weighing up to 100 pounds. Large quantities of fish were taken along the lakeshore until the 1940s, when the fishing trade dwindled.

The fishermen and their stories, for the most part, belong to history. When the lamprey eel took hold of the lakes, it spelled the end of good times for the fishermen. Large numbers of men fishing in tugs became a way of the past.

Hauling sturgeon at Grand Bend.

– COURTESY OF THE LAMBTON HERITAGE MUSEUM

The Sephie pulled down the St.Clair River by the tug James Reid, *1910.*
Large wooden schooners were built in Goderich from the 1860s.

John and Harriet Middleton with their family at the beach, Bayfield, c. 1900.

Chapter Seven

The Tourists Are Coming

FROM VERY EARLY, PEOPLE FOUND THE BEACHES OF LAKE HURON INVITING. They would come from the cities to spend several weeks at the hotels along the coast. The resort hotels were especially popular from the time they were constructed in the early 1870s, right up until the turn of the century.

An 1889 issue of the London *Free Press* remarked about Bayfield, "The large numbers who have been here pronounce it far ahead of other watering places." To stay at the River House, the Queen's Hotel, or the Albion Hotel cost about $3 a week, and the stage from Clinton to the railway station was free.

Boys could make 5 or 10 cents a day carrying water up the hill for cottagers. They also shovelled snow off the bridges for the sleighs, pulled flax, helped with the chores, and picked stones.

In 1875, it was decided that Goderich should have a temperance hotel, but because many of the shareholders refused to pay up, construction quickly came to a halt. However, the Huron House advertised, "Our best is good enough for you."

One of the more popular resort hotels in the Goderich area was Point Farm, J.J. Wright, proprietor. Guests came to Point Farm from all over. In July 1874, people from Montreal, New Orleans, Toronto, Detroit, Niagara Falls, and Massachusetts, as well as

A promotional postcard for the Balmoral Hotel, St. Joseph, 1907. The Balmoral Hotel was the most famous hotel on Lake Huron. Built by the popular Narcisse Cantin, the Balmoral was to attract tourists from all over the Great Lakes region. Furnishings were acquired at great expense from the hotel's more famous namesake in Montreal. Cantin was unable to raise the funds necessary to complete construction of the Balmoral, and it never opened.

– COURTESY OF NAP CANTIN

many local people (within a radius of 50 miles), registered for several days or a week.

The most prominent entry in Point Farm's guest list was the Royal family, who stayed during the 1875 season. Orders to the staff were that Royal family members were to receive all honours in accordance with their high rank. The flag was to be raised upon their arrival and lowered to half-mast upon their departure, at which time "the whole of the staff will assemble on the piazza displaying signs of sorrow."

After the close of the season in September, there were local parties. There was very little business in the winter, although the hotel remained open.

The Point Farm hotel could accommodate approximately 200 guests and board was $8 to $10 per week. Fare to Goderich was $6 by boat and $8.50 by Grand Trunk Railway. There was a telegraph machine on the premises and daily mail came from Detroit. A liveryman, A.M. Polley, ran a four-horse coach back and forth from Goderich to the hotel. He once described the coach dashing around the square, "swarming with living freight who were waving stars and stripes."

The Shield Hotel, Kincardine, 1895.
– COURTESY OF THE BRUCE COUNTY MUSEUM

The Bicycle Club at the River Hotel, Bayfield, c. 1880. From very early, vacationers flocked to the beaches along Lake Huron's Canadian shore.

– COURTESY OF ETHEL JOWETT POTH

Walker House, Kincardine, c. 1895. Kincardine's first hotel, the Walker House, was typical of Lake Huron's earliest moderately-priced summer hotels.

– COURTESY OF KINCARDINE LACAC

A cottage on the beach at Grand Bend.

– COURTESY OF THE LAMBTON HERITAGE MUSEUM

Cutters along Kincardine's
Queen Street, c. 1895.
– COURTESY OF KINCARDINE LACAC

Camping at Grand Bend, c. 1915.
By the turn of this century,
vacationers had stopped staying at
the resort hotels and begun to build
their own cottages. Often, families
would buy plots of land, pitch large
tents, and spend the summer
building their summer retreats.
– COURTESY OF THE LAMBTON
HERITAGE MUSEUM

Many local people got jobs at the hotel as cooks, maids and porters, but they considered the hotel pretentious, as it was much more expensive than Bayfield's hotels for instance, and rather grand in appearance, with three storeys and a portico. But J.J. Wright was a popular and charming man. He and his wife had previously run smaller hotels. Although all five mortgages were foreclosed on their hotel while it was being built, the notes were satisfied by selling off property around the hotel.

Point Farm's busiest period came just after it opened. As the years went by, fewer and fewer guests came for the summer season. The receipts for 1875 totalled $5,078 for the House and $705 for the Farm. Five years later, they were much less. A painstaking account was kept of payouts, including cigars.

Most hotels were not as large or as expensive as Point Farm, and many changed hands a number of times. Some had 25 to 30 rooms, complete with ladies' parlours, sitting rooms, a dining room for 50 or 75, a neatly outfitted bar, stable, sheds, and a yard. Some hotels were more popular than others, depending on their owners, a number of whom were legendary. Anthony Allen, of the Dunlop Hotel, was a huge fellow who could lift a man in each hand and crack their heads together. W.E. Elliott, a writer for the London *Free Press* and the Goderich *Signal-Star*, wrote that Allen stood 6 feet 6 inches and weighed 300 pounds. "If you came drunk to his tavern, you would get no more and out you would go — peaceably too, or Anthony's big foot would follow you out." Troublesome young men from Goderich would harass owners and patrons of the small taverns from time to time, but they left Anthony Allen alone.

The Bedford Hotel in Goderich had a cupola. Others had wraparound verandahs on two storeys. The hotels were the communication centres of their communities. Anyone sitting in a hotel bar soon found out everything there was to know about the town.

The grandest hotel on the eastern shore of Lake Huron was never completed. Called the Balmoral, it was built by Narcisse Cantin in St. Joseph to accommodate guests coming from Lake Erie on his proposed canal and electric railway. The hotel's ornately carved cherry furnishings were obtained from the Balmoral Hotel in Montreal, which had been remodelled. The hotel was reported to have an 80-foot bar, but unfortunately, it was built when the run on summer resorts was almost over.

Narcisse Cantin was an interesting character. One of ten children born in a log cabin, he raised his ten children in a 3-storey brick house with ornate woodwork and a

The Imperial Hotel, Grand Bend, 1912.

Students from Grand Bend Public School at the Fall Fair, 1921.

The Plaza Ice Cream Parlor was a popular summer spot, Grand Bend, c. 1920.

500-piece set of dishes that duplicated those of the French monarchy. Although Cantin was able to raise some money, he was unable to get government support for his canal and power schemes.

The Queen's, a small hotel across the street from the Balmoral, did a roaring business in St. Joseph during the town's two-year building boom. During the town's heyday, there was even a proposed St. Joseph-Stratford Radial Railway.

For years, large hotels such as the Sunset in Goderich operated only in the summer. The Sunset was finally torn down in the early 1970s.

Built in 1905, the Imperial Hotel in Grand Bend was the first hotel on the eastern shore to boast both cold and hot water in its rooms. It was three storeys, and rooms could be rented for $6 to $8 per week. All the hotels in Grand Bend were fully booked in the early 1900s.

Guests did not always find it easy to get to these shores, however, for they often became mired in the mud on the roads from London or the Pinery until well into the 1900s. As well, no matter how calm the waters of Lake Huron seem in the summer, or how inviting the beaches, danger lurks. The lake can become be storm-tossed in minutes. Many people unfamiliar with the strong undercurrents have drowned.

In Port Elgin in the early years, the Royal Princess Lodge boarded Toronto Maple Leaf hockey players. They worked out at the old arena in Port Elgin and on its fine beach. The lodge was originally built for people who came to get flour at the Mill Creek mill and for boaters. Mineral baths were developed and attracted people from all over. In the 1920s, rates were about $22.50 a week, meals included.

Guy Lombardo and his six-piece band opened at the Lakeview Casino in Grand Bend in 1919 for the July 1st weekend. Dance hall tickets sold for a nickel. Each ticket was good for one dance, and then the floor was cleared. This price was considered very expensive, but the casino was popular nevertheless. Liquor was illegal, but patrons were known to sneak in the odd bottle.

Opera houses and musicals were always full to capacity on their opening nights. Bathing beauty contests were held. Large gatherings such as picnics and fairs were held, with many thousands of people attending. Family reunions were held in the parks. Events such as candy-, cracker-, and bun-eating contests, pillow fights, and swimming races were held for the young people, while the older ones would sit around and talk. H. Pearson Gundy, author of *Those Summers on Lake Huron*, wrote that picnickers "would spread their lunch right under our noses. We had to rope off our lot with stout clothes-line, but even then they trespassed." Gundy spent childhood summers at his family's cottage in Grand Bend.

People gradually stopped staying at the large hotels. Instead, they bought or built their own cottages. Before the heavy periods of cottage construction, tents were pitched, creating white cloth cities. The first cottages were crude, with open studs and siding. Although they had no electricity or plumbing, they had iceboxes and beautiful pine floors. Early cottages could be built for as little as $90 and could be moved when the sleighing was good.

For the early cottagers, dances were held at pavilions and centres along the lakeshore. Once the summer was over, visitors took advantage of the hunting season for duck, squirrel and partridge, with varying degrees of success. Late in the fall, the cottages were closed up. With the approach of winter, the lake becomes too cold for bathing. Despite the departure of the summer people, local social life, often mixed with work, went on. There was sucker fishing, taffy parties, wood bees and maple syrup boilings to look forward to in the spring. The proceeds of a lawn social might come to $75.

In 1901, the Zurich *Herald* stated that Grand Bend was the most popular resort town on the eastern shore. All cottages were full and the cooks at the hotels were busy looking after the summer guests. As long as the projected Huron-Erie Canal was still being discussed in the papers, there was hope for the future. Questions such as when Narcisse Cantin was expected home, where he had been, and when he finally arrived were discussed in the paper. If there was a yearning for expansion and prosperity, there was also a sense of relief when things were quiet again. The locals were glad to see the summer people come, and they were glad to see them go.

The question of which area has the best sunsets has been debated for as long as anyone can remember. Goderich, Kincardine, Southampton and Grand Bend are all renowned for their colourful sunsets, so it is for the traveller to make up his or her mind.

In 1906, there was one cottage at Inverhuron. By 1968, there were over 300. In 1931, the Lime Kiln Lodge, a hotel and tearoom, was built for the locals and summer people. However, by that time most people could get about by car and the heyday of Lake Huron's large hotels was already over.

"It is dead here in the wintertime," remarked a local resident. The statement is as true today as it was then.

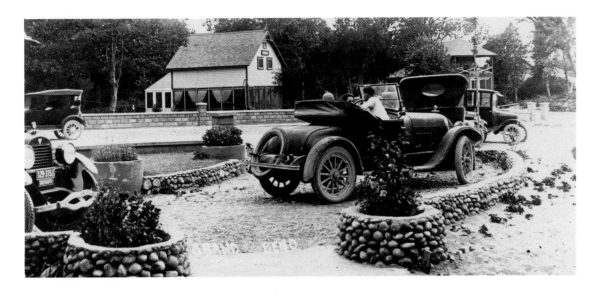

Looking across from the Lakeview Hotel to the Robinsons' cottage, Grand Bend, c. 1931.

— COURTESY OF MAC CAMPBELL

On the beach at Grand Bend in the 1940s.

— COURTESY OF MAC CAMPBELL

A view of the Lakeview Casino, the merry-go-round, and Schram's hot dog stand, Grand Bend, 1947.

— COURTESY OF PROVINCE OF ONTARIO AND MAC CAMPBELL

*The "Church Picnic," Grand Bend, c. 1920. Picnics and fairs
attracted huge crowds in the parks of Lake Huron's ports.*

Maurice Brenner's gas station, Grand Bend, c. 1930.

A bill from Brenner's Garage, 1943.
— Courtesy of the Lambton Heritage Museum

*Building the
Saltford Bridge, 1913.*
– COURTESY OF
THE HURON COUNTY
MUSEUM

Chapter Eight

Huron's Industrial Heyday: 1880-1900

The iron bridge over the Nine Mile River, Port Albert.

– COURTESY OF GENE C. McGEE

EVERY PORT HAD BUSINESSES AND FACTORIES that served the needs of its community. The population of the area along the lakeshore between Grand Bend and Southampton, including the towns, was about 15,000 in the 1880s. Though the Canada Company's ambitious plans to build roads and other amenities far exceeded its available capital, these towns prospered due to the enterprise of small-business men.

Once cleared, the area soon proved to be excellent agricultural land. Farmers quickly began exporting produce and livestock to market. In general, the growth of the towns was due less to manufacturing than to the need to provide services for the farmer.

In the town of Kincardine, bridge-building is an example of industry that was created in response to the needs of the community. The Hunter Bridge and Boiler Company began as a family business in 1879. The company built bridges in Kincardine, but they also had sidelines such as boiler installations and repairs. There was always a demand for Hunter's services because bridges had to be repaired after spring washouts. Wooden bridges were replaced by iron bridges, which in turn were replaced with concrete ones.

Salt and summer tourism were the main sources of revenue for the town of Goderich. It was reported in the newspapers that the first salt well in North America was at Saltford, north of Goderich. It was discovered by accident in 1866 while entrepreneur

Peter MacEwan was drilling for oil. At first, the brine was evaporated in the sun, but this method proved too slow. Then, a process in which boilers were placed below 80-by-20-foot pans was used to extract the salt. Many cords of wood were required to fuel the fires that burned 24 hours a day to heat the brine. In this fashion, about 100 to 125 barrels of salt could be made per day. It could be sold at $1.50 per ton for soiled salt and $2.50 per ton for clean salt, and was delivered to the railway cars in 300-pound barrels.

Repairing the Broadway Bridge after the 1917 washout.
– COURTESY OF KINCARDINE LACAC

Millinery store, c. 1900

The salt plant at Goderich, 1869.
– Courtesy of the Huron County Museum

Brickyards at St. Joseph, 1907. – Courtesy of Nap Cantin

The Canadian Pacific leaving Goderich, c. 1960. From left to right: Lou Fulford, Mike Hornblower Mr. Vines, and W.J. Chisholm
– Courtesy of Ken Chisholm

There were two different grades: table salt and dairy salt. Work began on the Manhattan Salt Mines, owned by H.Y. Attrill, in 1877. There were many other salt mines in the area at this time.

In Goderich, the Grand Trunk Railway arrived twice a day for mixed cargo and mail. Schooners arrived daily with 500 tons of coal for the North American Chemical Company and 150 tons for the waterworks. Huge rafts of logs, 700,000 at a time, would arrive at the port, bound for the new sawmill. Steamers were loaded apples, salt, horses and general merchandise. Schooners such as the *Sephie* carried lumber for the Ontario Lumber Co., as many as 18 loads of lumber and other supplies in one season.

In 1882, the steamers *Manitoba*, *Quebec* and *Ontario* called regularly at Goderich. Records of vessel entries were kept by both the harbour master and wharfinger for that year. In the November 1883 storm, in which dozens of boats were lost, the steamer *Erie Belle* exploded south of Kincardine while trying to free the schooner *Carter*. Four men were killed.

Schooners were at their peak just before the turn of the century, carrying goods such as staves and hoops for the cooper, and lumber, rails and ties for the railroad. But the triple-masted vessels were soon considered too large for the harbours and required too many crewmen.

During these boom years in Goderich, businesses asked for and received concessions from their towns. For example, the Goderich Organ Company asked for free water and nominal taxation for ten years, in view of their expansion. Soon, they were selling furniture around the world. In 1898, trade and growth in Goderich was estimated at just over $1,000,000.

From 1880 to 1900, even St. Joseph was a booming city, with a population of 150 souls and a floating population of many more. A new brick factory was under construction by the turn of the century, and a winery had just been built.

One local newspaperman noted that the Bayfield businessman could do well as long as he did not expect to make a fortune. Bayfield businesses listed in the 1884-85 directory included coopers, saddlers, carriage- and wagonmakers, blacksmiths, cabinetmakers and shoemakers. With general stores in the villages and mills down on the flats, such communities were almost self-sufficient.

Dreams of affluence made area residents lobby the government for new amenities.

In May 1896, meetings were held in Toronto for the Huron & Ontario Electric Railway project. Bayfield wanted a railway but soon realized that the community could not pay for even a fraction of it. The West Shore 999 train travelled to Kingsbridge from Goderich only two or three times before the route was abandoned.

At Southampton, the Mulberry Creek Oil Company struck a dry hole at 1,700 feet, after which representatives of the company made a hasty retreat. They had solicited local people to raise money and offered useless stock in return. The local people considered laying charges against the remaining representative, but when they discovered that representative knew nothing, they did not hold him responsible.

Port Elgin, situated on Lake Huron and Mill Creek, was a popular summer resort. The Wellington, Grey & Bruce division of the Grand Trunk Railway passed through here. Shipments from Port Elgin included grain, flour, sole leather, brushes, brooms and produce. The Port Elgin Brush Company employed as many as 60 workers. It was founded in 1883 and has not shut down one day since, except for stock-taking. The factory makes every type of broom and brush imaginable.

Lake Huron's businessmen took great pride in their two- and three-storey brick buildings, particularly those who had started in log-built stores and had built up their stocks, carrying everything from needles to anchors.

Others weren't as successful. The Kincardine Salt Prospecting and Manufacturing Company, after it struck brine, built its own kettle block to process salt. After several years its founders retired with "more experience than profit" and about $60,000 of idle equipment.

Kincardine was particularly proud of its large town hall, with a seating capacity of 600. The town had woollen and planing mills, a furniture factory, boiler and engine works, a stove foundry and other industries. By improving its port in 1875, Kincardine ceased to be an outpost of Goderich and became a commercial centre in its own right. It was also the northern terminus of the southern extension of the Grand Trunk. Access to the railway contributed greatly to the success of the small businesses in these ports.

By the end of the 1800s, transportation had improved in all the eastern lakeshore regions. A passenger could take a stage, coach, boat or train to Port Elgin or Goderich. The county roads were constructed of stone and were paid for by debentures.

At times, people were so eager to make a go of their communities that enterprise

The CPR station at Goderich

became the stuff of dreams. St. Joseph had an organ factory, sawmill, brickyard, novelty factory, and other factories in the early 1900s. Narcisse Cantin, raised $400,000 in a campaign to promote the town, a gigantic publicity scheme that he advertised in New York. He was determined to make Lake Huron the hub of wealth on the continent. Applications were made to Parliament for canals and electric railways from Lake Erie and Stratford, but no interest was shown. The government eventually built a small dock, which was hardly ever used.

An advertisement for the steamer Greyhound *in the* Huron Signal, *1907.*

The steamer Greyhound, *c. 1920. The* Greyhound *sailed regularly to Detroit. It provided moonlight excursions during its regular two-day stopover in Goderich.*
– COURTESY OF ETHEL JOWETT POTH

Picking apples near Bayfield, c. 1900.

Golfing near Kincardine, c. 1910.

Chapter Nine

Changing Lifestyles

A bill presented to Huron County for the body of a deceased person, 1861.

IN AN ASSORTMENT OF OLD PHOTOGRAPHS, there was one photograph of a small child, impeccably dressed, with half-open eyes. At first, it looked like all the other photographs of children from that time. But the child was upright, placed in a small white casket. The darkness of the lips and around the fingernails underlined a past in which a child's death was a common thing. Funerals took place in the home. Photographers attended these funerals, took pictures, and tried to sell them.

In the public records of any given community, birth, death and marriage records present a picture of the inhabitants' lives. Obituaries provide additional information, giving details of people's lives and offering remarks about their personalities. The dead were not always respected. Tombstones from pioneer graveyards, often located in the back fields of farmers' properties, were sometimes used as doorsteps by succeeding generations.

Sports and social events were well attended in the early days. There were cricket matches between the communities and golf was becoming popular. At picnics, every young man who was not occupied by the rites of courtship played baseball and cricket. They played hockey or curled in winter. The annual fair was not always a financial success, and by the end of the century, people had started to complain about the plank

John Middleton and Leila Feagan on their Wedding Day, 1917.
– COURTESY OF MABEL MIDDLETON

Fred and Mary Baker at their Bayfield frame house, c. 1910.

Bayfield girls at the river swimming hole, c. 1915. – COURTESY OF HARRY BAKER

John Young's Travelling General Store, Colborne Township, c. 1915. From 1908 to 1938, Mr. Young travelled Colborne Township peddling his wares from the back of his wagon. Mr. Young would serve people at their homes.
–DONATED TO THE HURON COUNTY MUSEUM COURTESY OF MRS. FRANK WILSON AND MISS RUBY YOUNG

An Old Boys' reunion in front of Patterson's Jewellery, Shoes and Harness Store, Kincardine, 1907.

seats. Nevertheless, the circuses and fall shows always brought out the crowds. The Bayfield Fall Fair in 1898 was described as being the best ever. It has not changed much over the years, with prizes being awarded for livestock, vegetables, crafts and baking. Kincardine's Fall Fair featured pipe bands, Scottish dances, various exhibits in the pavilion, and displays of animals.

Operas such as *Faust* were presented at the opera house for one night only. The shows featured gimmicks such as the "electric circle of fire" and the "electric skull." Local singers and violinists advertised in the newspapers and on posters, boasting about how well they were known. They toured the circuit of opera houses along with minstrel shows. A minstrel show was held at Port Albert in 1898 to raise money for the benefit of the town band.

Skating races were held but were not well attended if the ice was soft. On the other hand, the newspaper commented on the excellent water navigation sometimes right into January.

Regular mail service was established in 1862 between the ports of Goderich and Kincardine. Efforts were made for weekly as well as fortnightly postal service. Nowadays, mail takes five days to go from Goderich to Bayfield, a distance of about 10 miles. On land, the first mail was carried on horseback. Then the stagecoach took over. Later, the Grand Trunk carried the mail. Some early postmasters walked their routes, such as the one from Goderich to Kincardine. The stage brought the mail from Clinton to Bayfield until the early 1900s. Postmasters generally used their own homes as post offices, and people could come at any time to get their mail. The stage often had to cope with storms en route, and there were many accidents and delays. People felt that it was their right to ask the postman to get them a packet of tobacco while he was in town, and then drop it off on his way back. The postman's day might start at four in the morning, and it was filled with duties such as these. Nowadays, postmen in the region sometimes have to clean birds' nests out of the postboxes before they can leave the mail.

In the newspapers, there were columns with endearing titles such as the "Grist from the Local Mill" and "County News Served up to Suit Everybody." Lurid stories from afar competed with the local news. There were many advertisements for potions for women with bad nerves, and for Compton's cough syrup.

The larger ports, except Brewster (Grand Bend) and Port Albert, published their

The Currey family of Colborne Township, c. 1892. Large families were the norm around Lake Huron in the early days. A farmer needed all the hands he could get.

The members of the Bayfield Orange Lodge, c. 1920.

own newspapers on a weekly basis. Favourite topics were news from the "Old Country," wars, trends, and happenings in other centres. A very small portion of each paper was devoted to local interests. Advertising and pithy advice filled the rest of the pages, with the occasional "spectacular" — such as a local murder — thrown in for good measure. There were several murders in eastern lakeshore communities over the years.

In August 1899, the Goderich *Star* reported that "only those who have lived in a large town can realize the power of the home paper. Every bit of local gossip is read and discussed and sometimes it is a birth, sometimes it is a death, sometimes it is a marriage. Every name is familiar to all — for this reason alone the home paper is prized above and beyond anything the literary fellow can produce."

Not many newspapers survived pioneer publishing. Southampton's *Pioneer* folded after only three years, due to lack of support from the struggling community. Sometimes the papers would fail to print and would miss many weeks' news. Many papers, such as the Southampton *Morning Star* and the Bruce *Vindicator,* folded a few years after their inception. In Kincardine publications included the *Western Canadian Commonwealth* and the *Kincardine and County Bruce Advisor.*

In Goderich, the Huron *Signal* published for years. Port Elgin got the *Free Press* in 1869 and the *Busy Bee* in 1877. Newspapers changed names and ownerships many times.

The Ladies Sanitary Association gave out rules for keeping healthy. The good doctor could also be called, or the chemist would set people right with a dose of castor oil for irregularity or an embrocation for muscle stiffness. A dose of castor oil cost 18 pence.

Sometimes things would get out of hand. One doctor's bill, presented for the treatment an 84-year-old patient, came to 111 pounds 4 shillings. After 218 visits at 5 shillings each, the unfortunate patient had ingested 673 draughts of castor oil at 18 pence each, 54 boxes of pills and 2 powders at a shilling apiece. When the patient died, a bill was also presented for writing a certificate of death. Understandably, the patient's family was outraged. After much legal wrangling the bill was reduced.

It is easy to see why people sometimes preferred advice given in the paper to the administrations of a doctor. The newspaper offered advice on ways to commit suicide or, conversely, to keep one's health. They warned readers not to wear shoes and cotton stockings on damp nights or in cold rainy weather, and not to allow the love of gain to absorb one's mind at the expense of one's health.

After the turn of the century, there were new conveniences, such as cars, hydro electricity and telephones. A first, the new ways were upsetting. The transition from horse and buggy to car was gradual but the appearance of cars on the streets often startled the horses. In Bayfield in 1914, a team of hearse-horses were frightened by a car. The horses backed into the hearse, causing considerable damage.

The first several decades of this century were marked by divided opinions about these new conveniences. Some people had electricity, some did not; some had the telephone, some did not. Some were against the new innovations and some could not afford them. But everyone envied the first family on their concession to have a car.

Families were often large, with eight or more children, most of whom would find work in the cities, leaving only one or two to work on the farm, or to marry someone within the community. The rural areas around Lake Huron were particularly hard hit when the young people left the farms and moved to the cities. Those who moved away returned periodically to have a look at how things were going, and to remember. They would be upset if the house in which they had been raised had been sold or was not being looked after properly.

Memories of the past often centred around food and the way grandmother prepared it. Gooseberries and quince were made into pies, tarts and jam. Pound cake, tarts, sweet cake, ginger beer and raspberry wine were popular. "Mother and grandmother would make enough chokecherry and apple jam and jelly to last over the winter," wrote H. Pearson Gundy.

Life went on when the young men went to war. Lights were installed in towns, and ice jams caused fishermen worry. Dances were held at the pavilions, and young ladies waited to get married.

In 1914, styles changed. Skirts became longer and hats had feathers. Silk items, cashmere gloves, and satin undershirts were on sale that January.

There was a different social flavour in 1914, a civilized tone, with glee clubs, concerts, and meetings with the chairman of the school board.

By the time the area's concessions began filling up with cars, the small factories and the mills were had started to disappear. The small flour mills were closing down and grain was being shipped to larger centres. Industry was becoming centralized, and the self-sufficient community began to disappear.

*Florence Saunders at her
cookstove, 1910.*

– Photo by R.R. Sallows,
courtesy of the Huron
County Museum

By 1914, the move to the cities was well under way. Improvements in local travel and the railway contributed to this exodus. People left the farm for professions or factory jobs in the cities. They followed the jobs, went to war, or went out west to take up their own homesteads. As the towns and villages ceased to thrive, even more men went to other centres to find work.

The ports along the lake are now full of retired folk, and most of the young people who are raised here must go elsewhere to find jobs.

At the beginning of this century, many of those who didn't leave for the cities, but who saw little opportunity in their towns, found work in lumber camps. Alfred Ducharme of St. Joseph recalled his youthful activities in a lumber camp in his book *Nine Days on the Road*, which he wrote when he was 91 years old: "We walked nearly six miles before reaching camp. There was not much to attract us on our way except an occasional timber wolf crossing in front of us. There were tall pine trees on both sides of the road. At night in camp, we could hear the wolves howling."

Lumbermen relied on their feet to get them places. Coming by train to Goderich, Ducharme set out for St. Joseph, the old French settlement, but his feet were so painful and bleeding that he had to crawl the last section home.

Alfred's father, Joseph Ducharme, was born, lived and died in the same house in Drysdale. He raised 15 children. A blacksmith, he worked at the forge, making up to 50 horseshoes a day at 25 cents each. The family walked to Goderich and Seaforth to sell maple sugar and buy flour. The village of Drysdale once had a post office, hotel, general store, and several other businesses. It is now a ghost town.

Local men were very much involved in hunting and fishing, which they depended on to provide a portion of their winter food supply. Although area men still hunt, it is rarely out of necessity.

Most families were not as large as that of Mr. and Mrs. James Masse of Bluewater, south of St. Joseph. On February 16, 1937, their twenty-first child was born, and there were about 1,000 people on the lawn for the baptism. The Masse girls would peel one 11-quart basket of potatoes for the evening meal. One hundred pounds of potatoes would be purchased per week. Fourteen loaves of bread would be baked three times a week.

Many local people earned their living on the lake boats. One sailor, Captain Robert Wilson, went to sea at the age of 15. When he started in March 1930, there were still

Lumbermen, 1900. From left to right: Alfred Ducharme, Frank Denome, Frank Cling, and Frank Charrette. Frank Charrette was killed by a falling tree soon after this picture was taken.

Huron loggers, 1917. At the turn of this century, many young people who could not find work at Lake Huron's ports turned to the lumber industry for employment.

Mr. W.M. Henry at 79 years of age on his motorcycle, Goderich, 1937.
– Courtesy of Huron County Museum

Captain Bob Wilson on the Cedarton, *1936.*
– Courtesy of Bob Wilson

The Ducharme family, St. Joseph, c. 1942.
– Courtesy of Blaise Ducharme

two-masted sailing vessels: "The first thing you learned was how to fix the compass and mend sail." Captain Wilson made a career out of sailing, becoming a lake-boat captain and also sailing ocean-going vessels: "I was deep-sea before the war. Later, I was first mate on the merchant vessels in a convoy during the war." In the early days, he worked steamers such as the *Northton* as a deckhand. After the war, he was captain on a ship out of Halifax. He married his wife, Geraldine, in Halifax in 1938.

Port Albert in the 1940s.
– Courtesy of Gene C. McGee

The Cutter, 1909.

– PHOTO R.R. SALLOWS,
COURTESY OF HURON
COUNTY MUSEUM

Chapter Ten

The Old Folks at Home

MANY EARLY SETTLERS KEPT JOURNALS that vividly depicted their workdays, their trips to town, and their social lives. It was remarkable how mobile they were, sometimes going to town two or three times a week, to London for the theatre, or into Goderich to visit relatives. Whether by foot, by horseback, or by stage or sleigh, they always seemed to get to their destination.

In their journals, passages can be found about the digging of potatoes, fall ploughing, the brass band at the Christmas dance, and the price of goods purchased in town. They were very concerned about the weather. There are many references to spring, and most people could hardly wait for it to arrive.

H. Pearson Gundy, in *Those Summers on Lake Huron, 1900-1925*, wrote that to get to Grand Bend from Toronto, cottagers went to Parkhill by train, and then by horse and buggy to their cottages. Later, they drove Ford Jitneys. Upon arrival, they had the task of cleaning the cottage of mice and their nests, and airing it out for the summer. Gundy recalled many singular characters in the village during his youth. One such character was Mr. Brenner, who sat on his verandah from morning until night, chewing tobacco as he talked.

Bayfield strawberry pickers, 1947.   – Courtesy of Harry Baker

Murdoch Ross's sailboat with patched sails, Bayfield, 1915. Ross was an experienced sailor. Many times he survived storms when no one thought he could possibly return.
– Courtesy of
Ethel Jowett Poth

Harry Baker, Wilfred, and Daisy, 1919.
– Courtesy of Harry Baker

The old-timers were full of stories of the early days on the lakes — the wrecks, the storms, and the drownings. Boating on Lake Huron was treacherous, as sudden squalls would send huge breakers against the shore. The fishermen conjectured about where the hulks of specific wrecks were located.

Pioneers used the frozen roads and rivers as roads for their sleighs. When cars came into use, planks were placed across the frozen rivers to facilitate driving. People risked driving out on the ice until as late as 1935. "I could have lost the car that way," says Harry Baker of Bayfield, remembering people who drove out on the ice and were never seen again.

In the early days, lake transportation was by sail only, and you had to be careful when you were out in the lake. When the jib came around and knocked Murdoch Ross, a fisherman and Bayfield's first Sunday School teacher, into the water, his daughter Dolly had to pull him out and bring the boat into the harbour.

Gaelic was a dominant language of the Bruce in pioneer times, less so in Huron. Some Gaelic folk sayings that were commonly used by Lake Huron's settlers:

"There is always a fatness and a thinness in the seasons."
"Evenings are so short in the fall that they are like stones falling off a cliff."
"Friday was never a perfect day."
"The trend of a man is toward his name."

It could be said of the early settler that he lived in poverty more or less cheerfully, with an eternally optimistic outlook. Things would be better next year. In the French community, it was said that people even cheerfully paid their taxes. They endured every hardship imaginable, except flood, which they were usually safe from because of the high cliffs in their section of Lake Huron's eastern shore.

Many of the early farms in Huron and Bruce were started only to be abandoned. It was many years before the settlers had title to their lands. Many packed up and moved west or to the United States looking for something better. Of those who remained, many were self-taught and kept journals. One revealing pioneer journal was kept by a farm woman, starting with her marriage and ending three weeks before her death. Another settler made an entry once a year, at Christmastime, to record the year's happenings.

Kincardine's fire brigade getting ready for action, c. 1880.

A pioneer parade on Port Elgin's Main Street, 1900.

A section of this journal is included in the 1971 *Bruce County Historical Yearbook*. Its author died on Christmas Day with his pen in his hand. In 1861, he wrote, "I sot up a log house — and cleared tenn akers and put it in weet. Turble cold. Was chased out of the clearen by a pack of wolves yesterday." His life was a story of travail, illness and misfortune after his wife died. His son was killed in a barroom brawl and his daughter ran away with the hired man. Although he had personal difficulties, he had some success, buying extra land, a piano, and running for township reeve.

Life was hard. Many died young as a result of exposure, malnutrition or illness. The journals show that some people became very discouraged. Crops such as Indian corn, barley, oats, buckwheat, potatoes and turnips were grown, with yields of wheat running as high as 20 bushels to the acre. In the early years, the farmer was responsible for everything: providing schools, building churches, raising crops and livestock, fishing and lumbering. The farmer was a jack-of-all-trades. The farm wife made butter, cheese, wax candles and homespun cloth. After the 1870s, mills and factories began to supply such needs.

Today, the area has become one of the most prosperous farming areas in the country. The coastline is now completely settled with farmers who have sold off cottage lots from fields that abut the lake to raise extra money. The people who live along the coast are well aware that their own children will probably leave, as so many have in the past. They no longer dream that their towns will become great ports. They work hard to hang on to what they have, and to provide services for the tourists during those precious few summer months. In the town of Kincardine, which has a Scottish air, it is echoed: "Will ye no come back agin?"

Builders have long been advised not to build on the river flats, because periodically a river swollen by the spring run-off will carry away everything in its path — bridges, buildings, houses and mills. On a spring night in 1891, the swollen Saugeen carried away a lean-to in which two young girls were sleeping. The lean-to was swept out into Lake Huron and the girls were drowned.

Every year, a few swimmers are drowned, as they forget or underestimate the strength of the lake's undertow near breakwaters, piers and inlets.

Many men and women from the coastal area made their living on the Great Lakes, as cooks, sailors and captains on the lake freighters.

The Bayfield sewing circle, c. 1900.
– COURTESY OF ETHEL JOWETT POTH

John Kenny renovating a pioneer house, c. 1930.
– COURTESY OF
BERNADINE KINNEY

A picnic after mass at Kingsbridge Parish Church.
– COURTESY OF
BERNADINE KINNEY

In Gavin Green's account of his sailing days, he wrote that he left Goderich in 1885 by steamer, the *Ontario* or the *Quebec*, aboard which he paid $4.50 for his passage to Sault Ste. Marie. He slept on a grain bag on the deck. At the Soo, he could find no work. He was down to his last 25 cents, so he bought a 3-pound box of crackers. When he searched for a job on the boats, he asked, "Do you want to hire a man?" He found nothing. Later, he asked, "Do you want to ship a deckhand?" and got work. After eating crackers and water for three days, he was glad for a meal.

Settlers quickly made provisions for their churches. Early churches were small log or frame structures, perhaps only 20 by 30 feet. At first, most were Methodist churches, but as the population grew and churches joined together, brick edifices were built for various denominations. Around the turn of the century, a sizable brick church cost about $12,000. Many people in the community contributed land, money or labour toward the building of their churches. Once these houses of worship were built, members often had to walk up to 10 miles to attend their services. If one minister looked after several communities and no roads were open or other conveyances available, services might only be held once every several weeks. Visitors described the churches as tasteful and neat, and even the most basic structures often had doors and windows brought in from Toronto.

There was always a dance at Christmas, in a hotel, a shed or a barn. From journal accounts, you would think that a pioneer's life was a round of social events, extended visits, parades, dances, picnics and family get-togethers — a full schedule punctuated by hard work.

The shepherd, 1906.

The hull of the freighter Charles S. Price, *lost during the storm of 1913.*

Chapter Eleven

The Storm of 1913
and Other Storms

KEN FERGUSON, IN A 1956 ARTICLE in the Toronto *Star*, wrote about shipwrecks and storms: "Since Robert Cavalier de la Salle's *Griffon* vanished during a howling gale nearly three centuries ago, 10,000 ships have been estimated to have been swallowed by the Great Lakes." (The *Griffon* is believed to have sunk at the tip of the Bruce Peninsula near Tobermory or to have been destroyed by native attack in Lake Michigan.)

The accounts of wrecks off the ports along Lake Huron's eastern shore, the many dozen off Chantry Island and Kincardine's harbour are too numerous to record here. Often a blow would come up suddenly on the lake and schooners would get caught trying to run from one port to another, or would be dashed to pieces as they lay anchored offshore. Louie MacLeod, a Bayfield fisherman, could look at the calm lake and say, "It will be too rough for you." Sure enough, in an hour or so, the lake would be choppy, too dangerous for a small craft.

Steamers were supposed to be able to ride out all but the very worst of storms because of their great drafts. Their names tended to be sedate, giving the impression of being more stable than the more fragile sailing vessels. Steamers could take on heavy loads of supplies, foodstuffs or lumber, but often they shared the fate of the more fragile windjammers. They burned or were wrecked. The *Erie Belle* exploded while trying to rescue another boat in trouble.

In 1854, the *Bruce Mines*, a sidewheeler coming from Toronto, put into Goderich. The vessel routinely carried slag and ore to Toronto and brought back mixed cargo, including blasting powder. It was late November, but there was little wind. A gale suddenly came out of the west at about midnight, rocking the vessel. It eventually foundered off Cape Hurd as a result of a flash fire and an explosion. The *Bruce Mines* is featured in C.E. Stein's *Legends of the Lakes*, the story of a young man surviving a winter trapped beneath the ice in the sidewheeler's hull.

Every year, there were many storms that came up quickly, but none were as vicious or took as many lives as the storm of 1913. The captains of ships that survived it described 60-mile-per-hour winds that went one way while the waves went another. Freighters were broken in two, never to be seen again.

In the month of November, with the onset of winter and the increasing chance of sudden severe storms, the close of shipping draws nigh. However, in 1913 there were scores of bulk freighters on the lake trying to get a few last profit-making runs.

For two days, November 7 and 8, the storm raged. Then, on the 9th, reports of the disaster began to come in. The water had rose 4 to 5 feet above normal at the foot of the lake, seriously undermining the Fort Gratiot light, a beacon near Sarnia that helps ships steer into the St. Clair River. Heavy snow had accompanied the storm, making it impossible to see. With the lake frothing, almost as if it were boiling, tugs had attempted to leave the harbours to rescue vessels in distress, only to be turned back by the violence of the waves.

In all, 40 vessels and 235 lives were lost from Duluth to Toronto, the majority on Lake Huron. After the ships went down, debris and the bodies of sailors washed up on the Canadian side. Captains' books, diaries and life preservers washed up on shore as well.

On Tuesday, a farmer living near Grand Bend saw the body of a man drifting in the waves. Bodies drifted ashore all week, and eventually more than 60 were found on the eastern Lake Huron beach. Ten or 11 bodies were washed ashore north of Point Clark and were laid out in a Ripley funeral home. Among these victims were the captain, chief engineer and cook of the *James Carruthers*, a newly-built steamer loaded with wheat.

North of Kincardine, the *Hydrus* and the *Argus* were lost. Lifejackets from both boats were found on shore. A lifeboat from the *Hydrus* came ashore at Kincardine, with five men, all dead, lashed to its side. Wreckage and bodies came ashore here, drifting

NORTH CHANNEL

DETOUR
PASSAGE

MANITOULIN
ISLAND

GEORGIAN BAY

TOBERMORY

BRUCE PENINSULA

LAKE HURON

MICHIGAN
U.S.A.

JOHN A. MCGEAN
✗

ISAAC M. SCOTT
✗

SOUTHAMPTON

PORT ELGIN
DOUGLAS POINT
INVERHURON

ONTARIO

MATOA
✗

H.H. HANNA JR.
✗

HYDRUS
✗

ARGUS
✗

KINCARDINE
POINT CLARK

JAMES CARRUTHERS
✗

KINGSBRIDGE
PORT ALBERT

SAGINAW
BAY

WEXFORD
✗

GODERICH

REGINA
✗

BAYFIELD

NORTHERN
QUEEN

ST. JOSEPH

CHARLES
S. PRICE
✗

GRAND BEND

PORT FRANKS

GRATIOT LIGHT

SARNIA

*Locations of Lake Huron
shipwrecks and the ports along
the eastern shore. Many of
these wrecks were the result
of the 1913 storm.*

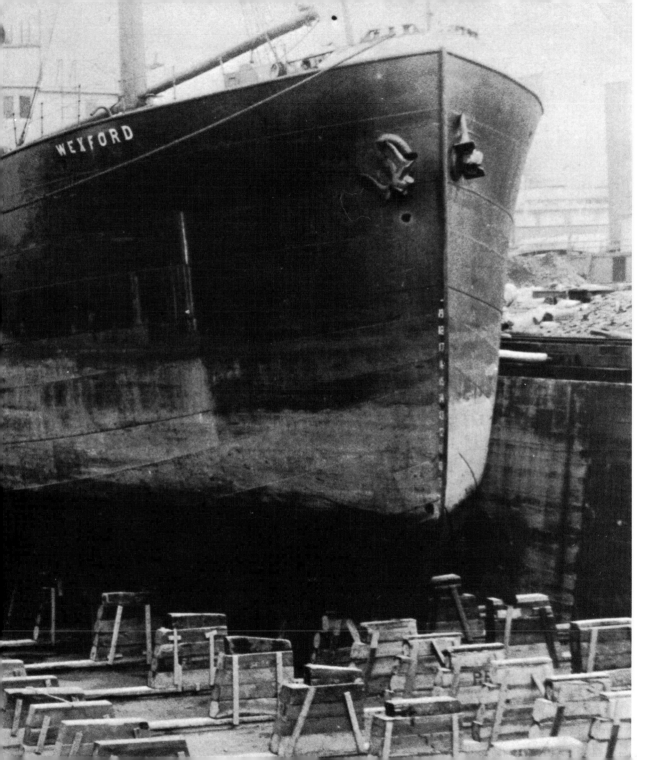

The Wexford, *built in England in 1883, was re-fitted in dry dock two decades later at Collingwood. The* Wexford *was thought to be indestructible. However, during the storm of 1913 it went down and all aboard perished. It is believed to be submerged near Grand Bend.*

down from Inverhuron, where residents had reported distress signals, flares and whistles late Sunday afternoon and night. Winds and currents carried away most of the crew and remains of the ships.

Traces of the *Price*, whose hull was floating upside down, were found near Port Huron, but nothing was found of the remaining ships. The crew of the *Hanna* was saved at Point aux Barques. All but the ocean-going *Wexford* were comparatively new. The *Price*, a bulk freighter with a wide, flat bottom, was considered to be capable of withstanding any storm.

The *Wexford* had weathered ocean storms and some claim to have heard its whistle off Goderich. It is believed to have gone down off Grand Bend.

It took more than a week to assess the damage the storm had done. On Lake Huron, it is estimated that eight ships went down, taking 178 men, but there may never be an accurate count of the dead, as many shipmates were unrecorded or known only by their nicknames. Mistakes in identification were made when people who had been recorded as dead later turned up alive. With the waters of Lake Huron churned up, wrecks from decades earlier were washed up on the beaches. Many dead men were found surrounded by debris, merchant goods and baled hay. In order to complete a reporting of bodies, $10 to $25 a head was offered. Relatives came from all over to the eastern shore of Lake Huron to identify the dead.

The storm left the entire area without communications. News was slow to come out of the communities, but they didn't need newspapers to know that boathouses and cottages had been ruined, forests blown down, and that their sheep and chickens had frozen to death in the fields.

When the storm was over and the large steamers had sunk, it was discovered a small wooden three-masted schooner, the *Sephie*, had miraculously survived. She was anchored with a load of lumber near the entry to Georgian Bay, apparently waterlogged but able to ride out the storm.

In addition to the loss of life, about $5 million in ships and cargoes were lost during the storm of 1913.

Today, with charts, separate lanes for lake traffic, buoys, lightships and weather forecasting, the risks have been reduced.

There were many, many other storms over the years. When they raged, ships that weren't able to make the western shore of Lake Huron would turn around and come back again. The *Azov*, a schooner built in 1866, was grounded on the beach near Sheppardton in October 1911 in similar circumstances.

It was a wonder that shipwreck survivors weren't frozen to death. Bob Wilson, a retired lakeboat captain, says: "Many times, during a late fall storm, a blow, you couldn't stay on deck. You'd freeze to death. If a ship went down, chances are another ship couldn't get there in time. The seas would be going over the breakwall." Wilson's father remembered the storm of 1913: "With the seas going over the range light, you could hear the whistle of an ocean ship laid off Goderich. She couldn't make it in and she went down with all hands."

Bert MacDonald, Goderich skipper and harbour master for 25 years, told a story about falling asleep at the wheel of a steamer. Returning from the Chicago World's Fair in 1892, he awoke at the wheel to find the steamer had cut a half-circle. He completed it to get back on course, hoping the skipper wouldn't notice. The next day, the engineer joked about it, saying that he could buy a couple of horses and train them on the half-mile track MacDonald had navigated the night before.

The MacDonald family have many interesting stories. Bert is credited with saving 60 lives during his career. He retrieved parts of the *Azov*, which was eventually lost off Chantry Island near Southampton. Bert's son Bruce said that saving lives was all in a day's work. An experienced seaman, he once saw a sailboat wallowing with her sail jammed fast. It was approaching the white waters of the reef, where it would almost certainly have flipped upside down, denying the sailor any chance of swimming clear. MacDonald took his *Wanderer* out, threw him a line, and hauled him to safety. Mac-Donald says, "And you know, that fellow just joked about it. To this day, he doesn't know how close he was to death."

Veterans had close calls, too. Boatbuilder Hughie MacLeod was saved by Mrs. Tudor Marks, who threw her shawl to him after his boat foundered and capsized on the long clay point in Bayfield.

A favourite pastime of old sailors is to speculate on why ships foundered and where they went down. The storm of 1913 is still a source of wonder and controversy: why ships like the small *Sephie* made it; how the crew was saved from the steamer *Northern Queen*, and how it ran aground a few miles north of Port Franks, the best place it could have struck.

Soldiers drill past the Walker House in Kincardine, c. 1865. From 1858 to 1870, the Fenian raids and the American Civil War were on the minds of most of Lake Huron's settlers. Although the region saw limited involvement in the conflicts, communities organized their own brigades.

Chapter Twelve

The War Years

LAKE HURON DID NOT SEE ANY ACTION DURING THE WAR OF 1812. No forts or defences were built along its coast, even though Gother Mann had surveyed the region for the British Admiralty in 1788. But during the Rebellions of 1837-38, in which settlers from both Upper and Lower Canada took up arms against British rule, some of the local farmers joined in. The most prominent of these men was Colonel Anthony Van Egmond. One of the founders of the Canada Company, Van Egmond owned the largest tract of farmland in the region. Before settling in Huron, he had served under Wellington at Waterloo. But once in Canada, Van Egmond became very active in the cause of settlers' rights. He was 67 when war broke out. Van Egmond was arrested for acting as a general for William Lyon Mackenzie, the leader of the rebellion in Upper Canada. He later died in a Toronto jail.

Despite Van Egmond's participation in the rebellions, for the most part, the local militia, with colourful names such as the "True Blues," the "Bloody Useless," and the "Invincibles," spent most of 1837-38 marching up and down the lakeshore.

The period around the American Civil War spelt both good and bad times for Lake Huron's settlers. The conflict brought a boom to the local economy, as farmers sold all

Air Navigation School No. 13 at Port Albert, c. 1940.

Jim Sherratt and Ernie Crocock, aircraft maintenance engineers of the Fleet Finch.
The Fleet Finch was a Canadian-built fighter plane that was used as an early trainer for
flight students around Lake Huron.

– COURTESY OF JIM SHERRATT

the grain they could produce. It was shipped to the United States along the Grand Trunk Railway, which had just been completed.

Of greater concern to many of the settlers in the region, especially those of Irish descent, were the Fenian raids. The Fenian Society was formed in 1858 with the aim of ending British rule in Ireland. Between the years 1866 and 1870, the Fenians organized raids in Canada to draw attention to their cause.

In Huron, a militia was organized to defeat the distant threat. In Bayfield, Irish farmer Mick Killip was so proud of the local militia scaring off the Fenians that he joked, "It was a lucky day for them when they got scared livers an' didn' come to fight, so me father and the rest of them heroes went to work clearin' up their farms."

Not all the settlements along Lake Huron's eastern shore were Irish. Scottish and Welsh settlements organized their own militia to defend themselves against the Fenians, or anyone else who might dare to attack in those volatile years. In Southampton, the colour sergeant drilled the volunteers. In Kincardine, the sergeant complimented his company on its rapid progress in drill and boasted that it soon would be one of the best in the country. For the most part, however, these measures were precautionary, if not alarmist; farmers in the region were far more interested in selling their produce than in becoming war heroes.

The ports were very active during World War I. In Southampton, in 1914, old vessels could be sold at a very high price, and orders came pouring into the ports for goods. In November 1914, the Goderich Knitting Company received an order for 2,080 dozen pairs of socks from the Department of Militia. Hundreds of horses were sent overseas. There was a need for other supplies as well. The American Good Roads Company of Goderich received an order on a few weeks' notice for 110 regular army transport wagons to be delivered by January 15, 1915. It meant that a full force of men had to work three shifts continuously until the order was filled.

During the war, business picked up in the coastal communities. In 1915, the Bank of Hamilton had assets totalling about $48.2 million, and 45.2 million tons of iron ore went through the Soo Canal. The production of wheat and grain was also up by millions of bushels. When Ontario Hydro took over the Bruce Power plant in 1930, it represented another boost to the area. That year, Southampton received its first shipment of coke, 550 tons to the Southampton Lumber Co.

Maintenance staff at Goderich Elementary Flying Training School No. 12, Sky Harbour, Goderich, 1941.

– COURTESY OF JIM SHERRATT

A restored Lancaster on display at Sky Harbour, Goderich, 1965.

By the end of World War I, economic activity had begun to settle to its previous levels. During the war, American ships had constantly called at the ports, but the mid-1920s most of the trade came from neighbouring towns. Before World War I, in 1906, most of the business done at Kincardine (22 vessels) was from the neighbouring ports of Goderich and Southampton. The thirties were an especially low period of activity at the ports. Only one British and one American steamer called at Kincardine in 1932. By contrast, in 1911, 22 schooners and 2 steamers had called. In 1934-35, one vessel, the *Mary Bob Roy* from Detroit, called at Southampton, compared to 1910, when 40 steamers called from Sault Ste. Marie. According to the port records of Goderich and Kincardine, the number of boats calling at these ports peaked during World War II, as many as 164 in one season.

Depression also marked the end of the schooner on the lake. Today, sailing vessels are seen as pleasure craft or are restored and called "tall ships."

As World War II approached, the residents of Lake Huron's shore communities prepared for involvement. In 1939, training camps were formed for infantry, artillerymen and pilots. The cliffs of Lake Huron were supposed to simulate the cliffs of Dover. Canadian-trained personnel were vitally important for the Allies during the Battle of Britain, but only a minority survived the war.

When Prime Minister Mackenzie King looked over his rather pathetic inventory of military equipment in the late 1930s, the issue of neutrality must have seemed very attractive. But, in 1940, when the government had to act, it did. The Air Training Plan was promoted by Air Marshall Billy Bishop, a Canadian hero and Victoria Cross recipient. He travelled the country assuring crowds that Canada would have an air force second to none. Considering the short time that they had to build camps and get personnel trained, it is amazing that they accomplished what they did.

The Air Navigation School No. 31 at Port Albert opened in November 1940 and closed in February 1945. Problems with mud, snow, and a lack of roads and buildings held up the program, but training continued nonetheless. British personnel at the base trained pilots and navigators who were destined for coastal locations in Britain. The British instructors were not used to the snowy runways and there are many tragic stories about training mishaps. Twenty-nine airmen were killed while stationed at Port Albert, either in crashes or by falling through the ice.

The Goderich Elementary Flying Training School No. 12 opened in October 1940 and closed in July 1944. The school could accommodate 70 pilots. A great number of young pilots were killed here too, most as a result of accidents that occurred during rigorous training runs. The fatalities were called the "wash-out rate."

"After someone flew their first solo, we would have a big party," an airman remembered. "There was no electronic navigation in those days. You flew by landmarks. If you got lost, you were told to fly west to the lake, then south to Grand Bend, and then inland."

Flying without instruments could be tricky. One airman, flying in a snowstorm, thought Kincardine was Bayfield, so he flew north looking for Sky Harbour, Goderich. When his gas supply was exhausted, he landed on a level piece of ice in Kincardine, at the foot of Lambton Street.

During one fog, a bomber crashed when its pilot tried to land in a flat field in the eastern part of Kincardine. The plane hit a rise in the land and crashed into a tree, killing two crewmen. Sometimes, if a plane could land on the ice, it could also turn around and take off on it.

Locals were hospitable. The pilots went to Grand Bend for dances and to swim, and they would rent cabins. Some of the airmen from other countries, such as Great Britain and the United States, married local girls and settled here, or took their new brides back to their homelands. Sometimes local boys joined the RCAF to serve as pilots or as radio operators.

A local girl remembers: "We would be out haying and when the yellow planes flew over, we would wave like anything and sometimes they would dip their wings. Dad used to blame the airplanes for the rain. He would say, 'Those dang airplanes bring the rain.'" Many of the local girls became enamoured with the dashing pilots. If they were seen holding hands or kissing under the streetlamps, their relatives would chuckle about it for years.

The romantic airmen were from out of town, but many of the local boys joined the army. The soldiers' pay per day (in Canadian dollars) was as follows:

THE SOLDIERS

PAY PER DAY (CANADIAN DOLLARS)	*1914*	*1939*
COLONEL	$ 7.50	10.50
LT. COLONEL	6.25	10.00
MAJOR	5.00	7.75
CAPTAIN	3.75	6.50
LIEUT.	2.60	5.00
2ND LIEUT.	-	4.25
WARRANT OFF.	2.30	4.20
Q.M. SERGEANT	2.00	3.10
COMPANY Q.M.	1.80	3.00
W.O. CLASS 3	2.75	-
COX Q.M. SGT.	1.70	2.50
SERGEANT	1.50	3.20
CORPORAL	1.20	1.70
LANCE CORPORAL	1.15	1.50
PRIVATE, TROOPER	1.10	1.30

While the boys were off at war, the people at home learned about rationing. In a supper to raise funds for a local library, the menu consisted of baked beans, baking-powder biscuits, and fresh russet cider. Coffee and tea were rationed during the war and were therefore not included on the menu.

Gasoline was also in such short supply that members could not get to the Bayfield Golf Club. Finances dwindled due to the falling numbers of golfers — many Bayfield summer residents didn't have enough coupons to get them to Bayfield and home again — and the club folded.

The number of living residents who took part in the war or who can remember the sacrifices that were made during those times sadly diminishes every year.

John Wain's farm, c. 1940

Bibliography

NEWSPAPERS:

Bayfield *Bugle*
Clinton *New Era*
Exeter *Times-Advocate*
Goderich *Star*
Goderich *Signal-Star*
Huron *Signal*
Huron *Expositor*
Kincardine *Reporter*

Kincardine *News*
London *Free Press*
Port Elgin *Times*
Southampton *Beacon*
Toronto *Star*
Toronto *Telegram*
Zurich *Herald*

MANUSCRIPTS:

Bayfield, Henry Wolsey, *Survey Notes*, 1816-1825.
Boyle, Anne, *Huron Historic Jail Report*, 1972.
Duncan, Allan, *Diary*, 1875.
Elliott, W.E., *Papers*, 1883-1980.
Goderich, Kincardine, and Southampton *Port Records*, 1910.
Gundy, H. Pearson, *Those Summer on Lake Huron, 1990-1925*, 1966.
Kingsford, W., Engineer in Charge of Harbours, *Letter-Book*, 1875-1876.
MacLeod, Margaret Fawcett, *Scrapbook*, 1925-1960.
Morrison and Edwards, Bayfield Merchants, *Journals*, 1860-1970.
Middleton, Leila Viola, *Journal*, 1917-1961.
Naftel, Alfred, *Journal*, 1876-1913.
Wilson, Captain Robert, *Scrapbook*, 1930-1980.
Wright, J.J., Prop., *Register Book, Point Farm, & Cash Book*.
Yemen, J.F., *Scrapbook*, 1925-1960.

PAMPHLETS:

Cantin, Narcisse, *Historical Sketch of Proposed Great Lakes to Ocean Route*, 1919.
Dixon, Andrew, *What Most People Don't See at Grand Bend*, 1963.
Salter, S.& Anderson, J., *Huron County Pioneer Museum*, 1980.
Women's Institutes, *Tweedsmuir Histories*, Grand Bend.
Wooden, J.L., *A Drum to Beat Upon*, Exeter, 1971.
    1875-1876.

BOOKS:

Robertson, Norman, *The History of the County of Bruce*, Toronto, William Briggs, 1906.
Levie, Carmen J., *Reminiscences: Port Elgin Centennial*, 1874-1974.
Gateman, Laura M., *Echoes of Bruce County*, St. Jacob's Printery, 1982.
Judd, Ann, Ed., *Bruce Township, Tales and Trails*, Bruce Township Society, 1984.
Courtney, Bob, Ed., *History of Huron and Its Hub: Ripley*, 1976.
Macleod, Norman, *The History of Bruce County 1907-1968*, 1969.
Smith, W.H., *Canada: Past, Present, and Future*, 1895.
Reynolds, John C., *Kincardine*, 1982.
Bruce County Historical Society, *Yearbooks*.
Wright, Jean Davies, *The River and the Rocks*, Auxable Bayfield Conservation Foundation, n.d.
Beecroft, Margaret S., *Windings*, Maitland Valley Conservation Authority, 1984.
Boyer, Dwight, *True Tales of the Great Lakes*, Dodd, Mead, & Co. 1970.
Boyer, Dwight, *Strange Adventures of the Great Lakes*, Dodd, Mead, & Co., 1974.
Fox, W.S., *Tain't Runnin' No More*, Oxford Book Shop Limited, 1958.
Fox, W.S., *The Bruce Beckons*, University of Toronto Press, 1952.
Mifflin, Mary Weeks- and Ray, *Light on Chantry Island*, Erin, Ontario, Boston Mills Press, 1986.
Great Lakes Fisheries Commission, *Commercial Fish Production in the Great Lakes, 1867-1977*, Ann Arbor, Michigan, 1979.
Ducharme, Alfred, *Nine Years on the Road*, New York, Carlton Press, 1969.
Magee, Gene C., *History of Port Albert No. 31 Air Navigation School*, 1987.

Parish of St. Joseph's, Kingsbridge, *Our Historical Heritage 1905-1980*, 1980.

Green, Gavin H., *The Old Log House*, Goderich, Signal-Star Press, 1948.

Green, Gavin H., *The Old Log School*, Goderich, Signal-Star Press, 1939.

Crawford, M., Ed., *Port Albert: 150 Years*, n.d.

Women's Institute, Dungannon, *A History of Port Albert, Dungannon*, 1980.

Huron County Historical Society, *Huron Historical Notes*, n.d.

Bayfield Historical Society, *Village of Bayfield History 1976-1985*, Zurich, AB Printing, 1987.

Wallace, Dorothy, Ed., *Memories of Goderich*, 1977.

Belden, H., *Historical Atlas of Huron County*, 1879.

Belden, H., *Historical Atlas of Bruce County*, 1880.

Roots and Branches of the Saugeen, Owen Sound, Stan Brown Ltd., 1984.

Scott, James, *The Settlement of Huron County*, Toronto, Ryerson Press, 1966.

Lobb, Alison, Ed., *The History of Goderich Township*, 1984.

Hazlitt, Shirley, Ed., *Colborne Connections*, 1838-1986.

Gazeteer, Goderich 1863-1864.

Gazeteer, Bayfield, 1901.

Folkes, Patrick, *Shipwrecks of the Saugeen 1828-1939*.

Industries of Canada: Historical and Commercial Sketches, 1890, The Railway and Steamship Pub. Co. of Toronto, Ltd.

Landon, Fred, *Lake Huron*, Bobbs Merrill, 1944.

Bush, Edward F. *The Canadian Lighthouse*, National Historic Sites Service, 1970.

Stevens, John R., *Lighthouses of the Great Lakes*, National Historic Sites Service, 1965.

Harris, R. Cole, Ed., *Historical Atlas of Canada, Vol. 1*, University of Toronto Press, 1987.

Williams, James N., *The Plan*, 1983.

Miller, Paul and Tremain, Robert, *Grand Bend: Images of Yesteryear*, Lambton Heritage Museum, 1988.

Kincardine Women's Institute, *Bruce County Tartan History*, 1975.

Albion Hotel and Main Street, Bayfield, c. 1940.